UNDERSTANDING INTERVENTIONS
THAT ENCOURAGE MINORITIES TO PURSUE RESEARCH CAREERS

SUMMARY OF A WORKSHOP

Steven Olson and Adam P. Fagen

Board on Life Sciences

Division on Earth and Life Studies
NATIONAL RESEARCH COUNCIL
OF THE NATIONAL ACADEMIES

THE NATIONAL ACADEMIES PRESS
Washington, D.C.
www.nap.edu

THE NATIONAL ACADEMIES PRESS   500 Fifth Street, N.W.   Washington, DC 20001

NOTICE: The project that is the subject of this report was approved by the Governing Board of the National Research Council, whose members are drawn from the councils of the National Academy of Sciences, the National Academy of Engineering, and the Institute of Medicine. The members of the committee responsible for the report were chosen for their special competences and with regard for appropriate balance.

This study was supported by Contract No. N01-OD-4-2139 (Task Order #172) between the National Academy of Sciences and the National Institutes of Health, National Institute of General Medical Sciences. The content of this publication does not necessarily reflect the views or policies of the Department of Health and Human Services, nor does mention of trade names, commercial products or organizations imply endorsement by the U.S. Government.

International Standard Book Number-13:   978-0-309-11226-0
International Standard Book Number-10:   0-309-11226-5

Additional copies of this report are available from the National Academies Press, 500 Fifth Street, N.W., Lockbox 285, Washington, DC 20055; (800) 624-6242 or (202) 334-3313 (in the Washington metropolitan area); Internet, http://www.nap.edu

Copyright 2007 by the National Academy of Sciences. All rights reserved.

Printed in the United States of America.

THE NATIONAL ACADEMIES
Advisers to the Nation on Science, Engineering, and Medicine

The **National Academy of Sciences** is a private, nonprofit, self-perpetuating society of distinguished scholars engaged in scientific and engineering research, dedicated to the furtherance of science and technology and to their use for the general welfare. Upon the authority of the charter granted to it by the Congress in 1863, the Academy has a mandate that requires it to advise the federal government on scientific and technical matters. Dr. Ralph J. Cicerone is president of the National Academy of Sciences.

The **National Academy of Engineering** was established in 1964, under the charter of the National Academy of Sciences, as a parallel organization of outstanding engineers. It is autonomous in its administration and in the selection of its members, sharing with the National Academy of Sciences the responsibility for advising the federal government. The National Academy of Engineering also sponsors engineering programs aimed at meeting national needs, encourages education and research, and recognizes the superior achievements of engineers. Dr. Charles M. Vest is president of the National Academy of Engineering.

The **Institute of Medicine** was established in 1970 by the National Academy of Sciences to secure the services of eminent members of appropriate professions in the examination of policy matters pertaining to the health of the public. The Institute acts under the responsibility given to the National Academy of Sciences by its congressional charter to be an adviser to the federal government and, upon its own initiative, to identify issues of medical care, research, and education. Dr. Harvey V. Fineberg is president of the Institute of Medicine.

The **National Research Council** was organized by the National Academy of Sciences in 1916 to associate the broad community of science and technology with the Academy's purposes of furthering knowledge and advising the federal government. Functioning in accordance with general policies determined by the Academy, the Council has become the principal operating agency of both the National Academy of Sciences and the National Academy of Engineering in providing services to the government, the public, and the scientific and engineering communities. The Council is administered jointly by both Academies and the Institute of Medicine. Dr. Ralph J. Cicerone and Dr. Charles M. Vest are chair and vice chair, respectively, of the National Research Council.

www.national-academies.org

PLANNING COMMITTEE FOR THE WORKSHOP ON UNDERSTANDING INTERVENTIONS THAT ENCOURAGE MINORITIES TO PURSUE RESEARCH CAREERS

ANTHONY L. DePASS *(Co-Chair)*, Long Island University, Brooklyn, New York
LARRY V. HEDGES *(Co-Chair)*, Northwestern University, Evanston, Illinois
DARYL E. CHUBIN, American Association for the Advancement of Science, Washington, D.C.
HOWARD H. GARRISON, Federation of American Societies for Experimental Biology, Bethesda, Maryland
CAROL B. MULLER, MentorNet, San José, California
KAREN KASHMANIAN OATES, Harrisburg University of Science and Technology, Harrisburg, Pennsylvania[1]

Staff

ADAM P. FAGEN, Study Director
TOVA G. JACOBOVITS, Senior Program Assistant (through June 2007)
REBECCA L. WALTER, Program Assistant (since June 2007)
JAY B. LABOV, Senior Advisor for Education and Communications

Consultants

STEVEN OLSON, Science Writer
PAULA TARNAPOL WHITACRE, Editor

---

[1] Dr. Oates retired from Harrisburg University of Science and Technology in summer 2007. In August 2007, she joined the National Science Foundation, Arlington, Virginia.

BOARD ON LIFE SCIENCES

KEITH YAMAMOTO (*Chair*), University of California, San Francisco
ANN M. ARVIN, Stanford University School of Medicine, Stanford, California
RUTH BERKELMAN, Emory University, Atlanta, Georgia
DEBORAH BLUM, University of Wisconsin, Madison
VICKI L. CHANDLER, University of Arizona, Tucson
JEFFREY L. DANGL, University of North Carolina, Chapel Hill
PAUL R. EHRLICH, Stanford University, Stanford, California
MARK D. FITZSIMMONS, John D. and Catherine T. MacArthur Foundation, Chicago, Illinois
JO HANDELSMAN, University of Wisconsin, Madison
KENNETH H. KELLER, Johns Hopkins University School of Advanced and International Studies, Bologna, Italy
JONATHAN D. MORENO, University of Pennsylvania, Philadelphia
RANDALL MURCH, Virginia Polytechnic Institute and State University, Alexandria
MURIEL E. POSTON, Skidmore College, Saratoga Springs, New York
BRUCE W. STILLMAN, Cold Spring Harbor Laboratory, Cold Spring Harbor, New York
JAMES REICHMAN, University of California, Santa Barbara
MARC T. TESSIER-LAVIGNE, Genentech, Inc., South San Francisco, California
JAMES TIEDJE, Michigan State University, East Lansing
CYNTHIA WOLBERGER, Johns Hopkins University School of Medicine, Baltimore, Maryland
TERRY L. YATES, University of New Mexico, Albuquerque

Staff

FRANCES E. SHARPLES, Director
KERRY A. BRENNER, Senior Program Officer
ANN H. REID, Senior Program Officer
MARILEE K. SHELTON-DAVENPORT, Senior Program Officer
EVONNE P.Y. TANG, Senior Program Officer
ROBERT T. YUAN, Senior Program Officer
ADAM P. FAGEN, Program Officer
ANNA FARRAR, Financial Associate
MERCURY FOX, Program Assistant
REBECCA L. WALTER, Program Assistant

Acknowledgments

Success of the workshop was dependent upon the willing participation of the many speakers and panelists, whose names are listed in the agenda in Appendix B, as well as the approximately 200 workshop attendees who shared their experiences and expertise. Speakers were also generous in making their presentations available for posting on the project website: <http://www.nationalacademies.org/moreworkshop>.

The planning committee benefited greatly from conversations with representatives from the Division of Minority Opportunities in Research (MORE) at the National Institute of General Medical Sciences (NIGMS), one of the National Institutes of Health (NIH), and, in particular, MORE division director Clifton A. Poodry, MORE program director Shiva P. Singh, and Rutgers University's Barry Komisaruk. In addition, representatives from those awarded grants in the first two rounds of the NIGMS Efficacy of Interventions to Promote Research Careers program met with the committee at a planning meeting held in August 2006.

In addition to its NIH sponsors, the committee and staff thank the Howard Hughes Medical Institute, for its sponsorship of an evening reception and other refreshments during the workshop, and the American Association for the Advancement of Science, for hosting the workshop and providing logistical support to the project staff.

This report has been reviewed in draft form by individuals chosen for their diverse perspectives and technical expertise, in accordance with procedures approved by the National Research Council's Report Review Committee. The purpose of this independent review is to provide candid and critical comments that will assist the institution in making its published report as sound as possible and to ensure that the report meets institutional standards for objectivity, evidence, and responsiveness to the study charge. The review comments and draft manuscript remain confidential to protect the integrity of the deliberative process. We wish to thank the following individuals for their review of this report:

Ella Booth, Oregon Health & Science University
Daryl E. Chubin, American Association for the Advancement of Science
Anthony L. DePass, Long Island University–Brooklyn
Kyle Frantz, Georgia State University
Howard H. Garrison, Federation of American Societies for Experimental Biology
Larry V. Hedges, Northwestern University
Jennie S. Hwang, H-Technologies Group and Asahi America, Inc.
Lyle V. Jones, University of North Carolina at Chapel Hill (retired)
Shirley M. McBay, Quality Education for Minorities (QEM) Network
Richard McGee, Northwestern University
Carol B. Muller, MentorNet
Karen Kashmanian Oates, Harrisburg University of Science and Technology
Georgine M. Pion, Vanderbilt University

Although the reviewers listed above have provided many constructive comments and suggestions, they were not asked to endorse the conclusions or recommendations nor did they see the final draft of the report before its release. The review of this report was overseen by **Willie Pearson, Jr.,** Georgia Institute of Technology, and **Enriqueta C. Bond,** Burroughs Wellcome Fund. Appointed by the National Research Council, they were responsible for making certain that an independent examination of this report was carried out in accordance with institutional procedures and that all review comments were carefully considered. Responsibility for the final content of this report rests entirely with the authors and the institution.

Preface

Even as currently underrepresented minority groups come to represent an increasingly large fraction of the U.S. population,[1] their proportion of biomedical and behavioral researchers has remained stubbornly low. In the biomedical and behavioral sciences, those historically underrepresented include, but are not limited to, African Americans, Hispanic Americans, American Indians (including Alaska Natives), and natives of the U.S. Pacific Islands.[2]

Of the 4,396 doctorates awarded in the biological sciences in 2005, just 158 went to African Americans, 227 to Hispanics, and 12 to American Indians.[3] African Americans account for 5 percent, Hispanics for 3 percent, and American Indians for less than 1 percent of the more than 600,000 full-time instructional faculty in higher educa-

---

[1] According to the latest U.S. census figures, African Americans made up 13.4 percent of the U.S. population as of 2006, Hispanics 14.8 percent, Asian Americans and Pacific Islanders 5.3 percent, and American Indians and Alaska Natives 1.5 percent. U.S. Census Bureau. Table 1. National Characteristics. Released May 17, 2007. <http://www.census.gov/Press-Release/www/releases/archives/cb07-70tbl1.xls>

[2] National Institutes of Health. *21st Century Scientists: Research Training Opportunities for Underrepresented Minorities* (brochure from the Division of Minority Opportunities in Research). <http://publications.nigms.nih.gov/more/more_info.htm>

[3] National Science Foundation, Division of Science Resources Statistics. 2006. *Science and Engineering Doctorate Awards: 2005*. NSF 07-305. Susan T. Hill, project officer, Arlington, VA. <http://www.nsf.gov/statistics/nsf07305/>

tion as of 2001.⁴ These percentages are even lower at the institutions that conduct the majority of the biomedical research in the United States. In 2005, barely 4 percent of the 3,951 faculty members in biological sciences departments at the 50 universities that received the most federal research funds in 2002 were African American, Hispanic, or American Indian—even though these groups currently make up more than a quarter of the U.S. population.⁵

For several decades, academic institutions, government agencies, and private organizations have implemented and supported a wide variety of programs designed to increase the number of underrepresented minorities who receive doctoral degrees in the biological sciences and become biomedical and behavioral science researchers. These programs have met with some success, and many minorities who are biomedical researchers today received critical support and encouragement from these programs earlier in their careers. Despite these past efforts to recruit and retain underrepresented minorities in the biological sciences, there remains a disparity between the representation of these groups in the general population and in the scientific workforce.

Among the programs designed to encourage underrepresented minorities to pursue scientific careers are those supported by the Division of Minority Opportunities in Research (MORE) at the National Institute of General Medical Sciences (NIGMS), which is part of the National Institutes of Health (NIH). Early in this decade, NIGMS decided to seek a better understanding of which aspects of individual intervention programs influence the progression of students toward research careers. It issued a Request for Applications (RFA) on the "Efficacy of Interventions to Promote Research Careers" that was designed to "support research that will test assumptions regarding the effectiveness of interventions that are intended to increase interest, motivation, and preparedness for careers in biomedical research, with a particular interest in those interventions specifically designed to increase the number of underrepresented minority students entering careers in biomedical and behavioral research."⁶

---

⁴U.S. Department of Education, National Center for Education Statistics, Integrated Postsecondary Education Data System (IPEDS), Winter 2001–2002. Data from 2003–2004 show similar patterns.

⁵D.J. Nelson. 2005. "The Nelson Diversity Surveys." Norman, OK <http://cheminfo.chem.ou.edu/faculty/djn/diversity/top50.html>.

⁶"Efficacy of Interventions to Promote Research Careers" (RFA-GM-05-009), released August 24, 2004. This RFA was reissued as RFA-GM-07-005 on June 9, 2006. RFA-GM-08-005 was posted on June 5, 2007.

In response to the RFA, NIGMS received 30 applications in 2003–2004; after thorough review, 6 of these applications were funded. In a second round of funding in 2004–2005, 26 applications led to 4 funded projects. In 2006–2007, 19 applications were received with reviews ongoing at the time of the workshop. A new RFA was issued in the summer of 2007, with applications due in October and new awards to be made in the summer of 2008.

The programs funded under the RFAs are seeking to understand the efficacy of educational interventions, some of which are described in this report. However, the reviewers of the applications found deficiencies in many of the unsuccessful proposals; these applications shared problems such as a lack of appropriate comparison or control groups, insufficient or inappropriate application of statistical techniques, or inadequate incorporation of pre-existing research and theories.

Recognition of these deficiencies was one of the factors that prompted NIGMS to ask the National Academies to organize a workshop to examine the current state of research related to interventions that influence the participation of underrepresented minorities in biomedical and behavioral sciences and other science, technology, engineering, and mathematics (STEM) disciplines. In addition, the workshop was designed to examine and generate research questions related to the topic, explore technical issues involved in carrying out this research, and encourage the development of an interdisciplinary community of scholars who are interested in understanding how to study what makes for effective programs to increase minority representation in the sciences. (The complete statement of task is included as Appendix A.) To be sure, a 1.5-day workshop could only just begin to introduce some of the issues that are part of this research. For example, although the brief technical assistance session addressed some of the most important methodological considerations for research in this area, there are many other challenges to conducting such research that were not discussed at the meeting and, therefore, are not included in this summary.

An ad hoc committee was appointed by the chair of the National Research Council to plan the workshop. (See Appendix B for the workshop agenda; biographical sketches for all planning committee members and staff may be found in Appendix C.) This workshop summary was developed by the designated rapporteur (S.O.) with assistance from National Academies staff (A.P.F.); the committee did not participate in the development of this workshop summary, although they had the ability to submit comments as reviewers.

The organizers of the workshop focused on research to understand interventions—what works and why—as opposed to the evaluation of intervention programs themselves. Research and evaluation studies can use quite similar designs, but they focus on somewhat different questions and, as a result, have somewhat different structures and different interpretations. Research seeks to identify the factors and practices that contribute to the effectiveness of an intervention, not whether the intervention succeeded. As planning committee co-chair Larry V. Hedges, Board of Trustees Professor of Statistics and Social Policy at Northwestern University, described the distinction, "program evaluations typically focus on the functioning and effects of particular intervention programs, while research on social processes focuses on understanding the mechanisms that bring about the effects of particular programs."

The success of this research is critical, said Anthony L. DePass, planning committee co-chair and associate dean of research and associate professor of biology at Long Island University–Brooklyn, because "one really wonders how much longer we have to get it right." In the 2003 Grutter v. Bollinger case, in which the U.S. Supreme Court upheld the affirmative action admissions policies of the University of Michigan Law School, Justice O'Connor wrote that "race-conscious admissions policies must be limited in time.... The Court expects that 25 years from now, the use of racial preferences will no longer be necessary to further the interest approved today."[7] This statement could be seen as motivating a paradigm shift, said DePass, "for us to look at other programs that are aimed at accomplishing greater diversity within higher education" and investigating them in a scholarly fashion. "There are political and other pressures for us to really get it right," DePass continued, "[to] create a body of scholarship that really demonstrates, based on empirical studies, what works, how to do it, and how not to do it."

The workshop planning committee, co-chaired by DePass and Hedges, was appointed under the auspices of the Board on Life Sciences of the National Research Council. The project was supported under a contract between the National Academy of Sciences and the MORE Division of NIH/NIGMS. The workshop was held May 3–4, 2007, at the American Association for the Advancement of Science in Washington, D.C., with approximately 200 participants; more than 100 other individuals had expressed interest in attending but could not be accommodated (even after moving to a larger space than was available at the National Academy of Sciences). The Howard

---

[7] 539 U.S. 306, 341-343 (2003).

Hughes Medical Institute provided additional sponsorship of an evening reception and other aspects of the workshop.

Although the focus of the workshop was on biomedical and behavioral sciences, very little of the discussion was specific to those fields—and much of the research presented was broadly applicable to other disciplines. In addition, several presenters mentioned that what is learned about underrepresented minorities may also be applicable to other populations or, in fact, all students. This summary, like the workshop, is addressed to a number of different stakeholders, including researchers and prospective researchers on the efficacy of interventions from a variety of disciplines; program directors and others involved with undergraduate research and mentoring programs; funders and other program supporters; individuals and institutions committed to recruiting and fostering the success of diverse student populations; professional societies; and others with an interest in these issues.

This workshop summary is based on a transcript of the meeting, and quotations are from the transcript. This document is written as a narrative rather than a strict chronology to highlight the major themes that emerged from the presentations and from the rich discussions that occurred throughout the 1.5-day meeting.

Any viewpoints expressed in this summary are those of the individual participants and do not necessarily represent the views of the planning committee, the National Academies, or the project sponsor. Speaker presentations, a complete list of registered participants, and other information about the workshop are available at http://www.nationalacademies.org/moreworkshop.

Contents

1 **The Nature of the Problem**   1

2 **Examples of Previous Research**   7
Social Cognitive Career Theory, 7
Human Capital Theory, 11
Social Identity and Stereotype Threat, 13
Survey Research, 18
Research on Existing Interventions, 20
Other Research Initiatives, 22

3 **The Elements of Effective Research**   24
Formulating a Research Question, 28
Designing Research Procedures, 30
Analyzing the Data, 34

4 **Developing a Research Agenda**   38
Pre-college Education, 41
Undergraduate Education, 43
Graduate Education and Postdoctoral Training, 46
Funders, 50
Building the Research Community, 51

Appendixes

A Statement of Task   55
B Workshop Information   57
C Biographical Sketches of Planning Committee and Staff   77

1

The Nature of the Problem

"We are faced with a really huge problem," said Clifton A. Poodry, director of the Division of Minority Opportunities in Research (MORE) within the National Institute of General Medical Sciences (NIGMS) at the National Institutes of Health (NIH). The scientific workforce responsible for advances in knowledge needed to improve human health and well-being is not representative of the general population. African Americans, Hispanics, American Indians, and other minority groups are severely underrepresented among the scientific workforce in general and among biomedical and behavioral researchers in particular. As Orlando L. Taylor, vice provost for research, dean of the graduate school, and professor of communication at Howard University, described the challenge, "research resides at the core of [U.S.] leadership and creativity and innovation. . . . As our demographics change radically in the country, and as the competition is changing radically, we know we cannot retain American leadership without greater participation by the full range of American people. . . . We must attract, retain, and graduate more persons from the groups that are the fastest growing groups in the country."

Greater diversity among the scientific workforce serves both abstract and immediate objectives, said Taylor. It demonstrates that the highest levels of achievement are accessible to the members of any group. It also enhances recognition of the full range of challenges affecting those in the United States, since minority researchers bring perspectives to their work that may not be common among non-minority researchers. "It is not just that you are fulfilling the American dream by bringing people in," said Taylor. Greater diversity also "enhances the talents of white and male researchers."

In his keynote address, NIH director Elias A. Zerhouni emphasized the importance of diversity to NIH's future. "The diversity of the scientific workforce has to be a reflection of the society within which it resides," he said. "Otherwise you end up with science becoming a sort of elite activity of a few, rather than the social activity that underpins the strength of society." In 2050, Zerhouni pointed out, more than half of the U.S. population will consist of minority groups that are currently underrepresented in science. "It is a strategic imperative that we succeed in making sure that we have the scientific body in 20 to 30 years that represents the vitality of our society."

Today's scientific workforce is a very long way from reflecting the makeup of the broader society. The representation of minorities within the pipeline leading to the PhD and to research careers drops at each successive educational level. In 2004, African Americans, who constitute about 13 percent of the U.S. population, received approximately 9 percent of the baccalaureate degrees at U.S. colleges and universities but less than 4 percent of the PhDs awarded to U.S. citizens. Hispanics, who constitute more than 14 percent of the U.S. population, received less than 7 percent of the bachelor's degrees and only a little more than 3 percent of the PhD degrees.[1] Even Asian Americans, though overrepresented in some fields, are underrepresented in others. In short, said Taylor, "there is quite a pool of people we are losing [from the pipeline]. We could double doctorate production by getting a good plumber."

Furthermore, even when underrepresented minorities earn PhDs, they appear to be less likely than white doctorate recipients to conduct research at elite research universities. In the 50 biology departments that have recently received the most federal funding, for example, the percentage of faculty members who are underrepresented minorities is less than the percentage of underrepresented

---

[1]Baccalaureate data: U.S. Department of Education, Institute of Education Sciences, National Center for Education Statistics. 2005. *Digest of Education Statistics: 2005.* NCES 0006-030. June 2006. Doctorate data: T.B. Hoffer, V. Welch, Jr., K. Webber, K. Williams, B. Lisek, M. Hess, D. Loew, and I. Guzman-Barron. 2006. *Doctorate Recipients from United States Universities: Summary Report 2005.* Chicago: National Opinion Research Center. (The report gives the results of data collected in the Survey of Earned Doctorates, conducted for six federal agencies—NSF, NIH, USED, NEH, USDA, and NASA—by NORC.)

minorities who received biology PhDs from 1983 to 1999, the pool from which most of the faculty is drawn.[2] As described below, faculty members from underrepresented groups may be more likely to "give back" to their communities and choose to work at a wider range of institutions.

Yet as small as these numbers are, a strong argument can be made that they would be even smaller without programs designed to encourage minorities to pursue advanced degrees in the biological, biomedical, and behavioral sciences. While the number of biological sciences doctorates awarded to white U.S. citizens and permanent residents stayed about the same from 1995 to 2005, growing from 3,115 to 3,337, the number of doctorates awarded to blacks rose from 107 to 158 (2.5 to 3.6 percent of the total), and the number to Hispanics from 127 to 227 (2.9 to 5.2 percent).[3] As David R. Burgess, professor of biology at Boston College, told the workshop participants, "a lot of the intervention programs you have participated in and directed and led have been very successful." Zerhouni agreed: "There is a sense that nothing works," he said. "I would submit to you that this is like saying we would have obtained the same results if those programs had not existed, and I disagree. I really believe that these programs have, in fact, facilitated the careers of many scientists who would not be successful today without these programs."

But there is a need to move beyond belief and anecdote, to conduct rigorous research that will identify the key elements that lead to successful programs. The real question, according to Zerhouni, is how to optimize the nation's investments in educational interventions. What interventions will have the greatest effect, and how much will those investments cost?

Both past and current programs have incorporated a wide variety of strategies. Some have been designed to remediate underpreparation. Others have sought to build the skills needed for success in research. Some have focused on building supportive learning environments. Many have provided financial assistance, and many have used research experiences as a way to achieve more than one of these objectives.

The obvious question to ask of these programs is "what works?" But that simple question is not very meaningful, according to Poodry,

---

[2]Donna J. Nelson. 2004. "Nelson Diversity Surveys." Norman, OK: Diversity in Science Association. <http://cheminfo.chem.ou.edu/~djn/diversity/top50.html>

[3]National Science Foundation, Division of Science Resources Statistics. 2006. *S&E Degrees, By Race/Ethnicity of Recipients: 1995–2004*. NSF 07-308. January 2007. Susan T. Hill and Maurya M. Green, project officers. Arlington. VA. <http://www.nsf.gov/statistics/nsf07308/>

"because the problem is a complex, multidimensional problem. What works to do what?"

In seeking to approach these issues, Poodry warned against what he called the "*n* of one"—each individual's preconceptions and understandings based on his or her own personal experiences. These experiences inevitably shape how a person sees the world. "If your conclusions concur with what people already believe, you are a genius," said Poodry. "If you contradict their *n* of one, you're a bum. I'll give you an example":

> Many faculty [members] and administrators tell me that minority science students, especially the financially disadvantaged, are far more attracted to professions—the MD—than to research careers, because of the potential earning power. What they tell me is that poor people, having been poor, are more concerned about making the most money.
>
> From my *n* of one, which includes growing up extremely poor on an Indian reservation, that is pure hogwash. I never knew a single poor person from a minority community who actually felt that way. Getting a good job as a nurse, a teacher, maybe an engineer, those were stretch goals. But the notion that we are going to do this to make the most money just wasn't part of my experience.

Overturning these "*n* of one" biases requires "some fantastic data and thoughtful analyses," according to Poodry. Asking interesting and answerable questions, designing persuasive research studies, and interpreting data appropriately will be necessary for convincing audiences that personal experiences may not always be correct.

In many ways, the existing programs have been "borne out of what we intuitively think," according to DePass. "We think if we put our students in a lab in the summer, it will make a scientist out of them—or it is going to move them to science. Have we studied exactly 'does it really work? Is that the best way to do it?' What environment, what other factors does one include with that to enhance success?"

Part of the problem in analyzing the development of the scientific workforce is the complex network of paths that people can follow to a research career, according to Jeremy M. Berg, the director of NIGMS. Prospective researchers hail from different kinds of undergraduate institutions and have had a wide range of experiences before college. They may become researchers through PhD programs, MD programs, or combined PhD-MD programs. Moreover, only some of those who earn PhDs in the biological sciences pursue research careers.

To fully understand how this network functions, three fundamental questions need to be answered, Berg said:

- First, *what* are the probabilities that an individual with a given set of characteristics will make the transition from one stage to another? Many kinds of transitions are possible, because of the multiplicity of paths people can follow to a career in research. And the probabilities differ for people of different races, ethnicities, and gender as they move along these paths.
- Second, *why* do people with different characteristics make the decisions that they do? Though many hypotheses seek to answer this question (as the next section of this report points out), only research can be expected to produce solid answers.
- Third, *how* can these probabilities be changed? Answering this question requires "a combination of understanding the 'why' and a very pragmatic understanding of what really works empirically," said Berg. "What sorts of interventions really have an impact? Are there interventions, say, at the college level, which not only influence the probability of going on to graduate school but also persist in encouraging increasing probabilities for an individual student going on to a particular path? . . . We need to understand much better what works. It is not just a question of program evaluation, but really understanding what interventions have real impact, how long it lasts, and so on."

A major challenge in answering these questions involves timescales, said Berg. Once an intervention is implemented, it takes a long time to gauge the effects of that intervention on the composition of university faculty. As a result, intermediate measures are needed to assess the program's effectiveness. "Five or six years along the way, even though you have not seen the impact at the end, you [need to] have some sense of what benchmarks to expect," said Berg. Having such benchmarks makes it possible to "monitor progress so that you are as confident as you can be that the program is likely to have the sort of impact that you intended in the first place."

Another major challenge is how to define success. Is a PhD student who goes to medical school a failure? "How can we be clear as to what our expectations are but also be realistic?" asked Berg. "If you say a hundred percent of your students should go on to PhDs, that is going to distort the program in such a way that you may end up hurting the overall outcomes."

A final challenge is determining the elements of a program that are working and those that are not. Researchers have to try to understand "what aspects of the program are the major and important contributors to that sort of success," according to Berg. This challenge is especially difficult, noted Zerhouni, given that social science research needs to deal with systems, and systems are often difficult to simplify in such a way that the effects of one part of the system can be isolated from other parts. "We cannot use the simple analogy of 'let's reduce the problem,' because by reducing it to certain parameters that everybody agrees to, you are losing, in fact, the essence of what the issue can be," Zerhouni said.

Today, social science researchers have not answered the three questions Berg specified. Even knowing what questions to ask and how to answer those questions can be challenging. "I am not so sure that I am hearing cogent analyses [or] powerful arguments about what are the real drivers," Zerhouni said. People have good will and want to have a fair and just representation of population groups involved in science, he continued, but the numbers are not changing as fast as many wish they would.

"So the charge [to the workshop] is simple," said Poodry. "What do we need to know in order to define effective interventions? What are the important questions? And what are the researchable questions? There are a lot of questions, but which ones can actually make progress with research? What kinds of research and what kinds of methodologies are needed to guide and test promising new interventions? . . . Today we want your help in focusing the questions that should be asked and your guidance as to the appropriate methods to answer them."

2

Examples of Previous Research

Researchers have examined the processes involved in decisions to study science in college, enter graduate school in the sciences, and become a scientist. These research programs originate in a variety of disciplines and can have quite different perspectives, but they also complement each other in explaining the complex processes involved in making educational and career choices. Because many of those interested in these questions are biomedical researchers who may not be steeped in social science viewpoints on these issues, the planning committee constructed an early session in the workshop to provide a varied set of lenses for participants to think more broadly about this kind of work—and to help consider themes for future study. The perspectives offered at the workshop—and in this summary—do not provide an exhaustive set, but they help to provide a broader set of questions and approaches for thinking about these issues.

SOCIAL COGNITIVE CAREER THEORY

Social cognitive career theory (SCCT) is an integrative theoretical framework that explores the psychological and social factors that produce personal interests and lead to choices related to education and careers. The theory is also concerned with the network of factors that affect performance and persistence in a person's educational and career paths and those that are responsible for an individual's satisfaction in a particular job.

Personal interests are not the only factors that drive educational and career choices and can be trumped by family expectations or other external influences. But interests are "strong motivational drivers of the choices that students make in their educational and career lives," said Robert W. Lent, professor of counseling and personnel services at the University of Maryland, College Park.

Lent described his work on applying SCCT to the issue of expanding the science, technology, engineering, and mathematics (STEM) pipeline, noting that it serves as a template with which to view and develop interventions designed to encourage minorities to enter research careers. SCCT draws heavily from the more general social cognitive theory of the Stanford University psychologist Albert Bandura. The key construct in Bandura's work is the concept of *self-efficacy*—people's beliefs about their ability to perform specific behaviors or actions. In particular, it refers to domain-specific confidence in particular situations, not to self-confidence as a general trait. In the context of science and mathematics, said Lent, self-efficacy addresses "the fundamental question: Can I do this thing? Can I, for example, do well in math and science courses in middle or high school? Can I do well in a science or engineering-related major in college?"

Self-efficacy beliefs, in turn, derive largely from four sources, according to Bandura's theory. The first and most important is prior performance—the levels of mastery or failure that people have experienced. "If I have done well in the past at a particular academic subject, for example, I am likely to expect in the future that I can do well in it as well," said Lent. "Conversely, if I've not done so well, my self-efficacy beliefs are going to drop."

The three other sources of self-efficacy beliefs are also important. One is observations of others' learning or the experience of models, especially models that one perceives as being similar to oneself. "For example, in terms of race, ethnicity, gender, social class, and so forth, viewing our models as being efficacious at things we want to do is a good way of raising self-efficacy—or lowering it, depending on the nature of the model," Lent said.

Another source of self-efficacy beliefs is the social messages that encourage or discourage participation in an activity. Students receive many messages from others and from the mass media that can influence their confidence about a particular activity. "But talk is cheap," Lent reminded the workshop participants. "Sometimes, if we try to convince people that they are good at things that we are not so sure they are—or that their own performance experiences disconfirm—then the source of that support may not be credible for very long, and people may not persist."

A final source of self-efficacy beliefs is physiological and affective reactions. For example, if a person is so anxious in taking every math test that he or she does poorly, that person is likely to infer that math is a personal weakness. "So test anxiety can be, in that example, a negative influence on self-efficacy," said Lent.

This is one way in which gender can influence self-efficacy beliefs in science and mathematics, Lent noted. In a general population of college students, women at the college level and below tend to report significantly lower self-efficacy beliefs at math compared with men. However, the same tendency is not exhibited in more specialized populations, such as engineering students. Also, if women have had similar experiences to men in terms of the four sources of self-efficacy beliefs, they tend to have the same self-efficacy beliefs as men.

Interest in Bandura's theory follows from a number of other factors, including the expectations surrounding particular outcomes. As Lent said, these beliefs "address the question: 'If I do this, then what will happen? If I major, for example, in science or engineering, or if I choose to pursue a research career, what will be the outcomes? What will be the payoffs for me, and what will be the negative consequences? What will the salary be like? What will my co-workers be like? Prestige? Autonomy?' These refer basically to career values that people want to fulfill."

Another factor is the goals that motivate people to engage in a particular activity or produce a particular outcome, such as trying to get an A grade in a particular math or science course. According to Lent, "Goals address the fundamental question of 'how much do I want to do this course of action?'"

Finally, within the theory, there are various kinds of social, financial, emotional, and other contextual supports and barriers that people encounter while pursuing their goals. These supports and barriers address the question of "'how will the environment treat me if I try this particular course of action,'" Lent said. For example, "the phrase 'chilly climate,' which oftentimes refers to the experience of women and certain minority groups in science and engineering fields, refers to the perception of environmental barriers."

The importance of self-efficacy beliefs is often obvious among students studying science and engineering, Lent noted. For example, he has seen many students who did extremely well in high school lose confidence when they got poor grades on their first college midterm examination. "All of a sudden their confidence levels plummeted, and they were convinced they were in the wrong field," Lent said. "They had never gotten Bs, or worse, before, and all of a sudden it was time to change majors and career paths."

The ongoing experience of success or failure subsequently modifies or stabilizes self-efficacy and outcome beliefs "in a never-ending loop," said Lent. Changes to these beliefs also can occur through outside influences like "technological advances, parenting, and other life experiences that may formulate changes in interest patterns because of their impact on self-efficacy and outcome expectations."

Each person has what SCCT theorists call "person inputs"—factors like personality, ability, gender, race, ethnicity, disability, and health status. These factors interact with background factors such as social class and the quality of early educational experiences. "Depending on who one is, and what one looks like, the environment may selectively provide or withhold certain opportunities," said Lent.

Lent and others have applied this framework in several major research projects. In a study of students at a predominantly white university, Lent and his colleagues found "that SCCT variables were well predictive of goals and actual persistence in engineering over a three-semester sequence."[1] This model was equally good at predicting choice and persistence goals in engineering majors when extended to two historically black universities.[2] Lent and his coworkers are now conducting a large-scale longitudinal study of computer science and computer engineering students at multiple predominantly white and historically black colleges and universities around the country.

This theoretical work has suggested particular intervention points and approaches, according to Lent. One possibility is to work at expanding vocational interests, especially in high-aptitude areas, and "getting people to rethink areas they might be able to do well at but have prematurely foreclosed upon because they don't believe they have the ability to do well or don't know enough about the field to want to pursue it." Other options are clarifying career goals, supporting career goals, strengthening self-efficacy, instilling realistic

---

[1] R.W. Lent, S.D. Brown, J. Schmidt, B. Brenner, H. Lyons, and D. Treistman. 2003. Relation of contextual supports and barriers to choice behavior in engineering majors: Test of alternative social cognitive models. *Journal of Counseling Psychology* 50: 458-465.

[2] R.W. Lent, S.D. Brown, H. Sheu, J. Schmidt, B.R. Brenner, C.S. Gloster, G. Wilkins, L. Schmidt, H. Lyons, and D. Treistman. 2005. Social cognitive predictors of academic interests and goals in engineering: Utility for women and students at historically Black universities. *Journal of Counseling Psychology* 52: 84-92.

outcome expectations, and helping people to manage environmental barriers and build effective support systems.

Past work has also emphasized how much more could be learned through further research that applies this model. A particular need, said Lent, is for more longitudinal, multiyear, and multisite research. Also, according to Lent, the basic theory needs to be studied in relation to women and underrepresented minorities in STEM fields, and more theory-based interventions and experimental studies are needed. "There has been some of this and I think it holds much promise for the future, but we need much more of it," said Lent.

Lent noted, by the way, that many individuals and groups outside of academia are interested in applying this approach to the issues they face. In addition to his university position, Lent is a visiting scholar at the U.S. Department of Homeland Security, and he said that the department views this issue as important to national security as well as economic prosperity. "There are some things that we probably don't want to outsource to other countries," Lent said.

HUMAN CAPITAL THEORY

Another theoretical perspective, this one rooted in economics, is known as human capital theory. As described by Anne Preston, associate professor of economics at Haverford College, each individual has a stock of skills, knowledge, abilities, and other characteristics that determine his or her wage-earning potential. Individuals can invest in increases in their own human capital through education, on-the-job training, and other activities. "Human capital theory basically allows us to understand under what circumstances an individual will decide to invest in further acquisition of human capital and [in] what types," said Preston. "So you can think of it as a pure cost-benefit calculation made by what we in economics always talk about—the rational and perfectly informed actor."

Of course, as Preston noted, "we do understand that not every individual is totally rational or perfectly informed." Costs, which Preston said are relatively easy to estimate, are for tangible expenses—such as tuition, room, board, books, and foregone earnings—and they occur at the time of the investment. Benefits, which can include future wages and future income streams, in contrast, can be much harder to predict.

In addition, these cost-benefit calculations often require discounting future income versus current costs. "Some people value future income differently than others," said Preston. "It depends on your current family income, maybe your family structure, the sorts of needs that your family has in terms of income now versus in the future, and the expected duration of the work life." Some of these factors can differ for different populations.

Finally, economists know that people do not always act in perfectly rational and perfectly informed ways. Methods exist to take a lack of information or irrational decision-making into account, but these methods may introduce additional levels of uncertainty.

Human capital theory can be used to provide insights into how interventions might lead to different decisions, Preston said. For example, mentoring programs can increase knowledge and change expectations. Better job placement programs might lead to better returns on an investment in human capital. Fellowships, research assistantships, teaching assistantships, and other forms of financial support can reduce the costs of the investment. Better information about the opportunities that investments give an individual can make a difference.

Methodologically, human capital theory is a strategy in which economists quantify variables and seek to determine the relationships among those variables. Some of these variables have discrete values, such as whether a person stays in a field or leaves it, or a person's race, sex, or type of school; others are continuous, like wages. Some variables are measured by proxies, as when the number of publications or number of citations are used as measures of research productivity. Preston explained that economists add variables to an analysis with the goal of explaining away the effect. If all variables that can be identified—except for the one under study—fail to explain away the effect, researchers have an indication that the variable under investigation plays an important role.

Economists also try to measure the quantitative effects of interventions. If mentoring programs are thought to make a difference, for example, economists will try to analyze whether being mentored influences the probability of investment in human capital. This could be done for majority and for minority students to see if there are differences in the effects of mentoring.

Studies such as this introduce what economists call "selectivity." If the individuals being mentored differ from those who are not mentored in some important way, the effect ascribed to mentoring may actually arise from personal characteristics, not the mentoring program. Economists can try to reduce these effects using various complex mathematical techniques, but Preston said that "personally, I find them not very reliable or satisfying." An alternative, she said, is "to move from these big national data sets [to create] individualized data sets." Approaches such as randomized trials, where individuals are selected to receive or not receive an intervention and the effects of the intervention measured, diminish issues of selectivity; however, they are seldom feasible and may even be unethical in such a setting, where some individuals are prevented from engaging in what is believed to be a positive intervention.

Another possibility is to collect data from natural experiments, using existing variation in the population of study. For example, student outcomes could be measured from different schools, some of which have an institutionalized mentoring system and others that do not. Such experiments require thought, time, creativity, and funding, said Preston, but "economists can really make some interesting inroads if they take up this challenge."

SOCIAL IDENTITY AND STEREOTYPE THREAT

Claude Steele, director of the Center for Advanced Study in the Behavioral Sciences, professor of psychology and Lucie Stern Professor in the Social Sciences at Stanford University, and his colleagues have focused their research on two main themes. The first is underperformance in school by groups whose abilities are negatively stereotyped in the broader society—an issue closely related to the persistence of members of these groups in pursuing research careers. The second is the set of broader issues posed by diversity. "It is one thing to integrate a school setting or work place," Steele said. "It is another thing to make that setting a place where everybody seems to flourish—where they feel like they belong."

Unlike many psychologists, Steele stresses the importance of context. "When we talk about schools and other environments of that sort, we tend to think of them as homogeneous environments—environments that are essentially the same for everybody. If there is one thing I hope you get from my remarks today, it is that they are different for people with different identities. The very same rooms with the same pictures on the wall, the same test items, the same teachers, can be very different as a function of social identities that a person has."

Each individual has many different social identities. These identities can be based on age, sex, race, religion, ethnicity, and so on. Different identities generate what Steele calls "contingencies"—reactions by others to a particular identity. "You have to deal with certain things because you have certain identities," he said.

An individual's social identities can change. During the great migration of African Americans from the southern to the northern United States, an estimated 10,000 to 30,000 African Americans "passed" from being "black" to being "white," asserted Steele. "[That's] what I mean by contingencies," he said. "They were avoiding the things that went with that identity." Another example includes changing a foreign-sounding name to one that sounds more American.

Some contingencies are threatening. An example might be an African American seeking to excel in an endeavor where members of that group are stereotyped as underperforming. When someone is threatened by the contingencies of a social identity, that person might seek to conceal or disguise that identity. But threats to an identity tend to make it central to your functioning, said Steele.

Stereotype threat is a good example of a contingency. Stereotype threat arises when a person is in a situation where a negative stereotype applies.[3] A good example is women in mathematics. In a series of experiments done by Steele and his colleagues, women and men who were equally skilled in math were given a very difficult math test one at a time in a testing room.[4] Women in this situation tended to underperform. When they experienced the frustration of a difficult test, the stereotype that women have weaker mathematical abilities suggested to women that they may lack ability. Men who are frustrated by the test may also believe that they don't have the necessary ability, but it's because of factors other than their maleness. "So for a woman in that situation, there is extra pressure—especially if that woman cares about math, has high expectations for her performance, or is committed to it," said Steele. In one recent study, simply mentioning the word "genetics" in the preamble to a math test worsened women's performance in math.[5]

However, when the researchers told the women before they took the test that "for this particular test, women always do as well as men," the women's performance was higher than when they were experiencing stereotype threat. Interestingly, the performance of men tends to drop somewhat under these circumstances. "We can be advantaged by stereotypes," said Steele, describing stereotype

---

[3]C.M. Steele, S.J. Spencer, and J. Aronson. 2002. Contending with group image: The psychology of stereotype and social identity threat. *Advances in Experimental Social Psychology* 24: 379-440. C.M. Steele and J. Aronson. 1995. Stereotype threat and the intellectual test performance of African Americans. *Journal of Personality and Social Psychology* 69(5): 797-811.

[4]S.J. Spencer, C.M. Steele, and D.M. Quinn. 1999. Stereotype threat and women's math performance. *Journal of Experimental Social Psychology* 35(1): 4-28.

[5]I. Dar-Nimrod and S.J. Heine. 2006. Exposure to scientific theories affects women's math performance. *Science* 314(5798): 435.

lift, in which one group can be "on the upside of somebody else's negative stereotype." Men may do worse on the test because "it isn't plausible to them that they lack the ability to do the work. It doesn't make sense. So the experience of frustration is less. If you take that advantage away from them, . . . then you may see some decrements in performance."

The effects of stereotype threat also were observed among African Americans taking a test using Raven's Progressive Matrices, a type of IQ test.[6] When told that the test was to measure IQ, African American students dramatically underperformed compared with white students. But when African American students were told that the test was simply a puzzle, their performance rose dramatically.

One remarkable finding from studies such as these is that the strongest students are often more susceptible to stereotype threat. "You have to care about [the domain] to experience stereotype threat," Steele said. "One protection against stereotype threat is not to care about it. [If you] dis-identify with the domain, then you don't care that much that your group is negatively stereotyped in that domain because you don't care that much about the domain."

These studies also emphasize the importance of cues in the environment that accentuate or lessen threats, Steele pointed out. "Cues that signal threatening contingencies foster vigilance," he said. "They hamper a sense of belonging in the setting, and this in turn impairs learning." One such cue is the number of other people in a setting with whom you share a social identity. For example, when women are greatly outnumbered by men in taking a math test, they tend to perform worse than if men are absent. This kind of marginalization through small numbers can have a powerful effect on identity threat. The profound segregation that exists on many college campuses can heighten a sense of difference.

The effects of cues on attitudes were tested in an experiment performed by Steele in collaboration with Mary Murphy, using students who were waiting to be interviewed for admission to a summer workshop on science and engineering. While waiting for the interview, they watched a videotape about the summer workshop that showed students working together. In one videotape, men and women were balanced one to one. In the other, men outnumbered the women three to one. The women who watched the video with the unbalanced genders had a much better memory of the inciden-

---

[6]R.P. Brown and E.A. Day. 2006. The difference isn't black and white: Stereotype threat and the race gap on Raven's Advanced Progressive Matrices. *Journal of Applied Psychology* 91(4): 979-985.

tal details of that videotape. Steele hypothesized that the cues in the videotape were making female viewers aware of their gender identity, which made them more aware of the situation than they would be otherwise. "Think of any time any of you have ever been in a situation where you are one of a kind," Steele said. "You pay attention." This awareness has effects not only on memory, but also on physiology. In fact, when the students were hooked up to physiological recording equipment (under the pretense that they would need it for a different experiment they would soon undertake), the women who watched the unbalanced videotape had much higher cardiovascular activity than the men.

Steele takes several messages away from this research. One is that these kinds of cues and reactions are virtually unavoidable in a diverse society such as ours. "Any diverse setting holds these identity threats," he said. "This is sort of an American challenge. I think at one level we should be proud of it because we are a society that publicly holds on to the idea that all of society should be integrated. . . . But one of the challenges behind that commitment . . . is making integration work. It is making these settings, these schools, these programs work for a truly diverse population."

Also, these cues do not arise solely from discrimination. On the contrary, he said, they can exist in the absence of discrimination. "These are contextual factors that make identities function in certain ways," he said.

The importance of cues also suggests ways to promote learning. If the cues change, performance can change. The most important change that has to happen, according to Steele, is for women and minorities to have a sense that they belong in a particular setting. "For instruction to work—and for the decisions we want them to make to be made—they have to have a sense of belonging. As a society, [we have to] understand that that has to come first." In fact, said Steele, without changing this sense of belonging, other interventions can be counterproductive: "If you push other things, like try to motivate [students], expose them to strong skill-focused programs, without at the same time addressing the sense of belonging, you can really get a backfire effect. Things may not work at all."

One cue is what people say. "What do the university president, the department chair, [and other] people say about the 'belongingness' of groups? Do they avoid the issue and see it as a minor issue and not something of importance? Or do they really own it and make the proclamation that everybody belongs intellectually in these settings?" he asked. Making the presence of particular groups the norm can relieve the tension in a setting and enable students to feel that they belong.

Similarly, a critical mass of people with a particular social identity is also pivotal, claimed Steele. Individuals are always looking around and counting how many other people share their social identities in a particular setting. "People do respond to numbers," he said.

Particular interventions can dramatically shape how students respond to cues. In a study done by Gregory Walton and Geoffrey Cohen at Yale University,[7] African American and white students watched and then discussed a videotape of an African American student talking about how alienated and out of place he had felt at Yale. But the student went on to recount how, during a trip home, his father reminded him what a superb opportunity it was to be attending Yale and that he needed to take advantage of it. The student described becoming active in a singing group and in academics, and he concluded that he was now very happy at Yale and that he was enjoying and learning from Yale's rich environment.

Just watching the videotape and talking about it raised the grade point average of African American students by two-thirds of a letter grade in the subsequent semester. "Why does that work?" asked Steele. "Because it gives [the students] an interpretation of the cues in the environment that [is] hopeful. . . . Everybody has those feelings [of not belonging], but if you're a group that the whole society negatively stereotypes in this way, those feelings are really a weight. So you need an interpretation that makes your sense of not belonging normal. This guy in the videotape makes it normal, and then he offers light at the end of the tunnel. Wow."

In another intervention, having African Americans talk with members of other minority and majority groups in informal settings greatly improved their grade point average. "They found out that things that were happening to them were not things that were just happening to black kids. They were happening to every kid. They got the data, the evidence that their experience was not racially based, and then when their experience was not racially based in this environment, the whole environment changed. It wasn't nearly as threatening. All those cues that might otherwise suggest threat were seen as much less threat." Steele recounted from his own personal experiences that having an advisor during graduate school who believed in him was enough for him to overcome the many negative

---

[7]G.M. Walton and G.L. Cohen. 2007. A question of belonging: Race, social fit, and achievement. *Journal of Personality and Social Psychology* 92(1): 82-96.

cues he encountered. "With this one big cue that said I did belong in that setting, the significance of the other cues tended to wane away," he recalled.

An especially powerful way to undercut stereotype threat is to attack and undermine people's theories of intelligence, Steele said, citing the work of Carol Dweck and Joshua Aronson. Many Americans tend to think that each individual has a particular level of intelligence and that one cannot perform beyond that level. But others, such as those from Asian and Eastern European cultures, see intelligence much differently. Students in those countries are more often taught that abilities are incremental and can be expanded through learning. They do not see math ability, for example, as something that is fixed and genetically determined but as something that people can improve. "I think this has huge effects on people's choices of majors and persistence in graduate school," said Steele. He felt that intervention on this topic would be especially valuable in entry-level, technical, and quantitatively based courses where students may receive their first sub-par grades, especially with faculty members who discourage students by telling them that many will drop out of or fail their courses.

SURVEY RESEARCH

Carefully conducted surveys can explore the attitudes, experiences, and thought processes that underlie the theoretical perspectives described above. With his colleague Catherine M. Millett, Michael T. Nettles, senior vice president and Edmund W. Gordon Chair of the Policy Evaluation and Research Center at Educational Testing Service, conducted a 28-page survey of about 9,000 doctoral students at 21 U.S. universities. (The research team used a variety of incentives to achieve a 72 percent response rate, Nettles noted, including a raffle for cash payments.) The survey asked students about their background, undergraduate and doctoral program experiences, finances, aspirations, and expectations for graduate study. Conclusions drawn from the survey were published in the book *Three Magic Letters: Getting to Ph.D.*[8]

One critical factor Nettles and Millett examined was how students are supported during their doctoral education. In particular, they contrasted fellowships (money, tuition, or fee waivers given to students with no expectation of repayment or of services to be rendered), research assistantships (tuition, fee waivers, or a stipend

---

[8]M.T. Nettles and C.M. Millett. 2006. Baltimore: Johns Hopkins University Press.

given to students with the expectation of research services to be rendered), and teaching assistantships (tuition, fee waivers, or a stipend given to students with the expectation of teaching services to be rendered). Nettles and Millett found that in the sciences, mathematics, and engineering, African American students were less likely than white students to be research assistants during their doctoral programs, even when background characteristics and student experiences are taken into account.

Yet being a research assistant can have a profound effect on a student's experiences in graduate school. For students with a research assistantship, Nettles pointed out, "we observe an increase in students' social interactions with peers, their academic interactions with faculty, their interactions with their faculty advisers, their presenting papers and publishing articles, and their overall research productivity." Somewhat surprisingly, a research assistantship did not influence students' time to degree, their overall satisfaction with their doctoral programs, or social interactions with faculty.

Nettles noted that universities often use fellowships to attract students to their institutions. While fellowships can be attractive to prospective students, they can have other consequences once students arrive on campus. Because students on fellowship are not always engaged in research or teaching activities from the beginning of graduate work, Nettles said, fellowships "can lead to the social isolation or the neglect on the part of faculty of students who are not actually engaged in the production of [that teaching and research]. . . . This is not to suggest that fellowships are not a good idea, but I think that what universities are experiencing is trying to figure out the right balance."

Another critical factor identified in the surveys is whether students have a mentor. Nettles distinguished sharply between an advisor—who acts in an official capacity to give a student advice about academic programs or coursework—and a mentor—who is a faculty member to whom a student turns for advice about intellectual and academic processes as well as general support and encouragement. One of the good messages to emerge from the survey, Nettles said, was that race was not a major factor in whether a doctoral student had a mentor (possibly the same person as a faculty advisor). Furthermore, of the students who had mentors, three-quarters were able to find them within the first year of their doctoral experiences. Having a mentor influences social interactions between students and faculty, unlike having a research assistantship. Having a mentor also influences the rate of scholarly publishing, degree completion, and even time to degree. However, it did not influence satisfaction with doctoral programs or whether students left the program.

A third key finding that emerged from their study was the importance of research productivity. Publishing in a refereed journal is a strong measure of this productivity, but the study showed that many other measures of research productivity are also important, such as presenting a paper at a research conference, publishing a book chapter, or being a member of a roundtable discussion at a professional meeting. As Nettles said, "many students pursuing research careers get on the train in different places." Over half of the students surveyed had presented a paper at a conference, published an article in a refereed journal, published a chapter in an edited volume, or published a book. Publishing in a journal "has become an extremely important endeavor for students," Nettles said. "In fact, many people feel that they can't complete [their degrees] without doing this because their first entry into the academic profession is going to be enhanced by their performance in conducting this activity."

However, the percentage of African American students publishing refereed journal articles in science and mathematics was significantly lower than for other groups (although that was not the case in engineering). Again, this was true even after controlling for factors such as student backgrounds and experiences.

Before doing the study, Nettles thought that research productivity might compete with time to degree because students would be devoting time and attention to producing articles and publishing. However, "we found just the opposite," he said. Publishing articles actually was associated with an increased rate of progress in their doctoral programs and reduced the time to degree.

RESEARCH ON EXISTING INTERVENTIONS

Existing intervention programs can have research components that produce broadly applicable information. An example is the Alliance for Graduate Education in the Professoriate (AGEP), funded by the National Science Foundation. Yolanda S. George, deputy director for education and human resources at the American Association for the Advancement of Science (AAAS), which has provided evaluation capacity-building activities and research resources for the AGEP program, explained that the goal of AGEP is to increase the number of underrepresented minority students pursuing advanced studies, obtaining doctorate degrees, and entering the professoriate in STEM fields, including the social sciences.

AGEP has identified several factors that facilitate progression of minorities into STEM post-secondary studies:

- Taking high-intensity and high-quality advanced high school STEM courses
  - STEM pre-college programs
  - Post-secondary support programs in core STEM courses
  - Financial aid packages that reduce debt burden
  - STEM pre-graduate-school bridging programs.

The institutions that participate in AGEP "are expected to engage in comprehensive institutional cultural changes that will lead to sustained increases in the conferral of STEM doctoral degrees, significantly exceeding historical levels of performance," George explained. She discussed several of the important lessons AGEP has demonstrated in seeking to achieve this goal. One lesson, according to George, is that admission and selection committees need to be conscious of diversity issues. The AGEP program tries to have a diversity coordinator or diversity-conscious faculty member sit in on admissions and selection. "You will get a behavior change if you get an advocate there," said George. AGEP programs have also found that following up with applicants and linking financial aid to admissions helps with recruitment.

At the same time, AGEP has found that it is important to work closely with university administrators on what can and cannot be done with recruitment and retention programs. George said, "You have to start talking to counsel about diversity-conscious and legally defensible student admission selection criteria, financial aid, and programs before you get that letter from that group that is threatening to shut you down." Furthermore, these discussions need to be ongoing, said George, since challenges will continue to arise.

AGEP has conducted meetings and workshops to explore particular topics. For example, a 2003 meeting on mentoring found that relatively little was known about mentoring specifically for STEM students.[9] "We know that STEM core mentoring appears to be more prevalent in the after-school programs at the middle and high school level, but the level of systematic STEM career and workforce mentoring is not high in undergraduate research programs," George said. However, support networks for women, including students, in STEM areas in academia, industry, and government are useful in

---

[9]AAAS created a Science Mentoring Research website that followed on the 2003 meeting: <http://ehrweb.aaas.org/sciMentoring/>.

helping to balance family and career, negotiating organizational or departmental challenges, and advancing in a career.

George also observed that, through its program evaluation capacity-building project, AAAS has helped AGEP awardees build comprehensive evaluation and assessment infrastructures to examine their graduate education enterprises. The framework for making change includes collecting and using disaggregated data for decision-making and leadership development within the faculty and administration. The goal of AAAS's AGEP program is "to help the leaders in these projects, [who] are the deans and provosts in some cases, faculty members, and people who run the program, to figure out how to evaluate and assess the infrastructure in order to get the types of effects that they want," George said. A particularly important task is to help faculty and administrators understand the research that has been conducted so that they can engage faculty members in the process of institutional change.

OTHER RESEARCH INITIATIVES

Several other important lines of research were mentioned more briefly by presenters and attendees at the workshop. Two described here are conducted by current grantees of the Efficacy of Interventions program; additional interventions and research studies are discussed elsewhere in this summary.[10]

For example, Reba Page, professor of education at the University of California, Riverside, conducts ethnographic studies of mentoring, journal clubs, research in labs, and so forth to understand how those components of intervention programs play out in practice. She wants to know "not what do people tell us they are, not what does the brochure tell us they are, but what do they actually look like in real time, as people, students and teachers together, enact the components." By studying these situations and the processes they entail, Page is able to examine "the assumptions that undergird those processes and what holds them in place, and what we might want to target if we wanted to change them." A prominent question in her work is why outcomes seem so resistant to change. The conclusion she has drawn is that outcomes depend not only on the culture of science but on the culture of the broader society. To understand science, including science education, "we have to see that science is embedded in our society," Page said.

Another line of research focuses specifically on the attitudes

---

[10]See, in particular, Chapter 4 for discussion of initiatives by educational stage.

and preferences of students. Merna Villarejo, professor emerita at the University of California, Davis, has asked students in interviews about the motivating factors that caused them to make particular career decisions. Students who went to medical school tended to say that they want to give back to the community. But "that is not what researchers say," Villarejo observed. "The most frequent answer for researchers for 'why did you choose your profession' is 'because I really love science; it just turns me on; it is exciting; it is great.'"

According to Rick McGee, associate dean for faculty affairs at Northwestern University's Feinberg School of Medicine, another distinguishing characteristic was between students who wanted a fairly predictable future and those who were willing to live with more uncertainty. The students most likely to go into research were the ones who said, when asked about their future, "'I don't know, I might be doing this, I might be doing that, I might do this for awhile, I might do that for awhile.' . . . They really are quite different people," McGee said.

As Daryl E. Chubin, planning committee member and director of the AAAS Center for Advancing Science and Engineering Capacity, said, many kinds of investigations can produce information needed to advance minorities in research careers. "Where does knowledge come from? We know it comes from data and we know it comes from research. But it also comes from evaluation and it comes from technical assistance and it comes from first-person reports. . . . The challenge here is to learn from all of these interventions and then try to apply that in our own context."

3

The Elements of Effective Research

One of the most applied sessions of the workshop featured a series of presentations on planning and conducting research on the effectiveness of interventions. Describing these methods in a single session is "taking on the impossible," acknowledged committee co-chair and session moderator Larry V. Hedges of Northwestern University. Students spend a significant portion of their time in graduate school studying these issues. Nevertheless, the organizers of the workshop hoped to at least introduce the major topics that researchers might consider before undertaking this work.

To begin the session, Shiva P. Singh, program director in the Division of Minority Opportunities in Research (MORE) in the National Institute of General Medical Sciences at the National Institutes of Health, gave an overview of the historical context under which the 2003 Request for Applications (RFA) was developed, namely the continued underrepresentation of minorities in biomedical and behavioral sciences. He then outlined some of the major questions that the RFA was meant to address, such as the following examples:

- Can specific forms of teaching, styles of pedagogy, and mentoring be identified that prompt patterns of student engagement that lead to a biomedical or behavioral research career?
- Are some characteristics of a student more determinative in career choice? Are some characteristics more subject to intervention?

- Can an optimum window for intervention be identified either by student age or level of maturity?
- Can behavior patterns critical for a successful biomedical or behavioral research career be taught effectively?
- Can the influence of mentors or other role models be measured, linked to outcomes, and modified?
- Do research experiences (including collaborations at majority institutions) positively affect career choice, and what are the principal components of these experiences and effects?
- With respect to the decision to enter (or remain in) a research career, can the influence of peers, family, community, and economics be distinguished, measured, linked to outcomes, and modified?

Singh provided data on the research community's response since the RFA's 2003 inception, including the number of applications received and funded. He discussed changes that the division has identified since 2003 designed to improve the program. One is to be clearer about what the RFA is designed to produce. "We are interested in empirical—rather than evaluative—research that produces generalizable lessons that may be useful in promoting greater participation of underrepresented minority students in biomedical and behavioral research," Singh said. He also underscored the importance of future applications' incorporating a sound, theoretical basis for the hypothesis to be tested; a sample with sufficient statistical power; appropriate comparison or control groups; and rigorous statistical methods.

The division also has come to emphasize the importance of a team approach. As Singh explained, "you need people who know how to run a program, people who know how to ask questions, and people who know how to design an experiment and analyze the data. . . . So a team approach [is necessary]: a collaborative effort among researchers, program administrators, educators, psychologists, sociologists, statisticians, and economists."

The intention of the RFA was to test the assumptions on which the division's grants were based, said Barry R. Komisaruk, associate dean of the graduate school, professor of psychology, and Board of Governors Distinguished Service Professor at Rutgers University and, in addition, a program director in the MORE Division when the RFA was being developed. Do laboratory experiences, mentoring, academic enrichment, and other interventions really stimulate students to enter careers in biomedical and behavioral research? If so, how do these interventions exert their effects? "What we hoped and we continue to hope is that this research will provide insights and modifications in program practices that will increase the entry of students into biomedical and behavior research careers," Komisaruk said.

Komisaruk offered examples of a number of questions that he described as "fundable," in that they attracted the attention of reviewers and program officers in previous rounds of competition:

- What were the critical motivating factors—both positive and negative—among those who pursued biomedical research careers as well as those who did not, despite participating in intervention programs?
- Among recent undergraduates, which factors and experiences affected their decision to enter or avoid a biomedical career, such as the nature of the interactions with their mentors or research experiences?
- Among graduate students in the biomedical and behavioral sciences, what were the optimal times of their entry into a research laboratory experience, and what are the characteristics of these students and their experiences that may have contributed to their pursuit of graduate study?
- How are career decisions influenced by providing information to students on the skills necessary for success, such as formulating research questions, laboratory management, bioethics, publishing, grant writing, and scientific presentations?
- Do hands-on laboratory experiences and laboratory skills acquired as undergraduates affect entry into graduate school?
- How do students' perceptions of the social culture of a research-intensive university versus a university that is more balanced between research and teaching affect their career choice?

Komisaruk also described some of the major questions reviewers asked of these applications:

- Is the proposed program research, or is it an assessment or description of a program?
- Is there a clear rationale for the study? For example, is there a testable hypothesis, or is it just observation?
- What is the likelihood that the proposed intervention will have a measurable effect? For example, is the duration of the intervention that is proposed so short (minutes, a day, or a brief summer session) that it is unlikely to have a measurable effect on the outcome?

- Are the outcome measures a valid indicator of whether the student will eventually go into a biomedical research career? For example, if the student is given a summer experience or a week-long experience to increase interest in the field, does this produce a long-term effect six months later on the career interest expressed by the student? If it does produce increased interest, does that result in an increase in entry into graduate school or a career?
- Are the comparison groups appropriate and ethical? If you apply an intervention to some and you don't apply it to others, are the latter being deprived of a beneficial treatment? Those who want to go into a program may differ in motivation from those who do not actively seek out and choose a program. Which are the appropriate comparison groups—those who are accepted into a program but decline, those who are accepted but cannot participate because of space limitations, or those who are not accepted?
- Is the research sensitive to the unique social, cultural, economic, and other issues of the groups being studied?
- Are women and minorities being lumped into the same categories, even though the issues affecting them may be significantly different?
- Is the design of the questionnaires and interviews appropriate? Are the questionnaires validated? Are the statistical analyses and other analytic techniques appropriate?
- Are the conceptual basis and the relevant literature for the proposed research made explicit?
- If it is a multicomponent intervention, how is a critical element identified? For example, how do you differentiate the effects of mentoring versus social support versus research?
- How do students' involvement in other programs and activities affect their responses to the program being studied?
- In focus groups, how do investigators address the possible social pressure against revealing what one doesn't like? Students may not want to say what they don't like about the program if they are in the focus group.
- Are the research findings generalizable to other programs?
- Will the data obtained from the research program be manageable? For example, a study with 500 hour-and-a-half interviews would generate an enormous amount of qualitative and quantitative research data.
- Are the interview questions unrealistic? For example, the veracity of recall for adults asked about their elementary school experiences could be questioned.

- Does the principal investigator have a track record with this type of research? If not, does the research team have the necessary expertise?
- Is the measured outcome relevant? For example, does the number of publications really relate to successful career entry into the field?
- Has the principal investigator responded adequately to an initial critique of the grant request?
- Does the proposed study compromise confidentiality?
- Is the principal investigator sufficiently involved in the research?
- Is the application a strategy to fund a program rather than a proposal to do research?

FORMULATING A RESEARCH QUESTION

Formulating a good research question is a topic "that you could say with truth is never taught, and you could say with truth that it is constantly taught," said Martin M. Chemers, professor of psychology at the University of California, Santa Cruz. Given the "presumptuousness" of trying to speak for all researchers in addressing this topic, Chemers generalized from his own experiences in developing a research project to study minorities in the fields of biomedical and behavioral research. In particular, he emphasized three things that research needs: focus, theories, and competencies.

Educational interventions are exceedingly complex. They involve activities associated with the intervention, things that might be measured to see if the intervention is working during the intervention or shortly after, intermediate outcomes, long-term effects, and so on. "You can't study all of this," said Chemers. "You have to focus, you have to pick some piece of it to study." In choosing how to focus a study, researchers almost inevitably peer through the lens of their own expertise. In Chemers' case, his past work had been focused on leadership—specifically, on people's beliefs about their ability to be a leader—so he brought this focus to his research. In a study of first-year college students at UC Santa Cruz, he and his colleagues focused on the role that academic self-efficacy played in the students' performance, health, and adjustment.[1]

The second point Chemers emphasized is that "without a the-

---

[1] M.M. Chemers, L. Hu, and B.F. Garcia. 2001. Academic self-efficacy and first-year college student performance and adjustment. *Journal of Educational Psychology* 93(1): 55-64.

ory, you don't know what to study among all the things that you could study." Kurt Lewin, the father of modern social psychology, once said that "there is nothing so practical as a good theory." For Chemers and his colleagues, this meant developing a framework, or rubric, describing the central features of programs designed to affect the decisions of minorities to enter or not to enter biomedical and behavioral research. In their research, the central theory was that the psychological drivers of these outcomes are related to a student's belief in his or her ability to do research, which the researchers called "inquiry self-efficacy." Later, they also sought to measure the extent to which a student felt a sense of belonging and had an identity that was compatible with being a scientist.

They also hypothesized that the role of these factors varies by ethnicity and gender and initiated somewhere from six to eight studies to study this question. "Each one of them," said Chemers, "had a weakness that couldn't be escaped." In one study it may have been difficult to find controls, in another the short-term outcomes were difficult to measure, and so on. Their approach was to have the studies overlap, with the methodology of one study at least partly correcting for a problem in another area. "If the results held true over and over again in all these different methodologies, it increased our confidence that what we were finding was real and valid," Chemers said. They used interviews, case studies, surveys, longitudinal studies, and other research techniques. For example, they longitudinally followed two cohorts that spent four weeks on campus each year as part of a high school science program. They also looked across 14 different programs on campus that support underrepresented students in science careers. They also sought to probe the abilities students acquired as part of their education. In one set of measures, they had students engage in simulations that measured their ability to take a set of data, analyze those data, draw conclusions, and recognize the assumptions and limitations underlying those conclusions.

The breadth of Chemers' research highlights the third point he made: "Unless you already know everything, which is rare among many of us, bring the relevant expertise to your team." When he received the RFA from the MORE Division, said Chemers,

> [I]t rang a bell. It had a common overlap with things I had already done. But I recognized that [my previous research] was only one piece of it, and there were a lot of other areas that fit in, that were either related to efficacy or were outcomes of efficacy, where I wasn't an expert. So I brought in people. I elicited help from people in the natural sciences to help me identify the nature of scientific

inquiry in the natural sciences. I brought in people who were expert in scientific learning assessment.... I brought in a specialist in mentoring. Finally, I enlisted the support of a statistical consultant, a faculty member in my department who was very good at this. So even though I have been a social psychologist for 39 years and done many, many studies, it was clear to me that I didn't have the range of skills for myself that would do this.

The research team was divided into subgroups with overlapping memberships that met more frequently than the complete team. "It is like leading an army," Chemers said. "We have faculty from psychology, education, chemistry and economics. We have graduate students from psychology, education, chemistry and earth sciences. You want to talk about cultural differences—you have some vast cultural differences between the social sciences and the natural sciences."

Nevertheless, Chemers stated that he believes there is no difference in the basic scientific method between the social sciences and the natural sciences. In both areas, "rigor means that there can't be competing explanations for what you find. You have to design a study so that at the end you can say, 'this is what we found,' and when people say 'it might have been this, it might have been that,' you say, 'no, we controlled for this, we measured that, it can't be those things.'" Even though the social sciences and the natural sciences may use different methods, "the point still holds that controls help you know whether what you found is accurate."

"One of the most valuable pieces to this entire study was that we developed an atmosphere of mutual respect" among scientists from different disciplines, Chemers said. "We could ask questions about each other's work. We could say 'I don't see how that works,' and we were open to hearing."

This research "has been one of the most complex and challenging projects that I have ever been involved with—and also one of the most exciting and most rewarding," Chemers concluded.

DESIGNING RESEARCH PROCEDURES

Research design has two integrated components, said Hedges, who gave the presentation at the workshop on designing research procedures: (1) a strategy for data collection and (2) a coordinated strategy for data analysis and interpretation that is designed to answer research questions. In that regard, research design needs to be tightly coupled with the formulation of the research question. "In fact, one of the great weaknesses of research proposals that I have seen—not only in this program, but in others, as well—is the failure to tightly couple problem formulation and research design and analysis," Hedges said. "When you bring together a team of people and have one person write each of those three sections, you very often get a proposal in which those don't articulate very well."

Research design requires creating a "logic of inquiry," according to Hedges, that explicates how the empirical evidence being collected implies an answer to a research question. This logic of inquiry needs to be situated within a knowledge base, since, as he noted, "you have to start from somewhere" and make explicit why the collection of a particular set of data is relevant to the question. "The logic of inquiry provides a kind of argument about how empirical evidence is going to be used to shed light on the research question," said Hedges.

The logic of inquiry can rely on qualitative or quantitative measures and often involves a mixture of the two. It can rely either on intensive designs that try to capture a lot of empirical evidence about a relatively small number of people, or on extensive designs that collect a smaller amount of data about a larger number of people or a larger number of programs. As also described by Chemers (above), effective research designs often combine elements of different approaches to make up for the weaknesses of each approach.

Research design needs to adhere to several fundamental principles, said Hedges, ideas that are "so simple in some ways that I wouldn't mention them except that I have seen proposals blunder in each of the areas that I am going to mention":

- First, variation is essential in order to obtain empirical evidence that relations exist. If researchers study only effective programs, they cannot be sure which features of effective programs do not also exist in ineffective programs. Some variation occurs naturally, while other research designs create variation, as when experiments or quasi-experiments are conducted. Many designs, Hedges pointed out, are hybrids that involve some naturally occurring and some artificially created variation.
- Second, not all relations are equally sized. "To understand whether or not an effect which might lead to designing an intervention is worth paying attention to," Hedges observed, "you need to know how big it is." The size of an effect needs to be compared to other effects or measures to gauge its importance. "Without knowing that, it is hard to say whether that so-called treatment effect is big enough to take seriously or so small as to be unimportant," Hedges said.

- Third, according to Hedges, when studying developmental processes or the effects of those processes, longitudinal studies are almost always more revealing than cross-sectional studies. "Studying the same people over time and not different groups of people who happen to be different ages has been incredibly important in various areas of social research, and revealed things that weren't known before," Hedges said. A classic example is the study of poverty in the 1960s, where cross-sectional comparisons largely overlooked the fact that many people cycle in and out of poverty, which leads to quite different understandings of what poverty is and how to address it.

In looking for the causes of particular effects, Hedges pointed out that Thomas Cook and Donald Campbell of Northwestern University and William Shadish of the University of California, Merced, have developed a framework for thinking about research design.[2] Their framework involves four classes of validity: statistical conclusion validity, internal validity, external validity, and construct validity of cause.

- *Statistical conclusion validity* focuses on whether the relation between variables observed in a study is accurate. For example, are the measures being used reliable enough to permit the relation to be observed in the first place, are the analytic methods appropriate for the kind of data that were collected, and were the assumptions made by the analytic procedures met in the data collection process?
- *Internal validity* asks whether a relation between variables is causal or just an association. The classic example is the relation between ice cream sales and the monthly homicide rate in major cities. The two are not causally related, but they both increase as temperature increases. "In the warm months, people eat a lot of ice cream and they also commit a lot of crimes, but that doesn't mean that the relationship between ice cream sales and crime is causal," said Hedges. Another way in which the internal validity of a design can be compromised is when different treatment groups have different kinds of students. "If the best students wind up selecting themselves into an intervention, the intervention is going to look better than it deserves to look in a certain sense, unless you find a way to take that into account," Hedges said.

---

[2]W.R. Shadish, T.D. Cook, and D.T. Campbell. 2002. *Experimental and Quasi-Experimental Designs for Generalized Causal Inference.* Boston: Houghton Mifflin.

- *External validity* involves generalizability. If an intervention is identified as causally related to an outcome, would that relation generalize to other settings and other individuals? For example, if researchers work in a setting that is very unusual or with participants that are highly unusual, the results may not generalize.
- *Construct validity of cause* asks whether the "active ingredient" in an intervention has been correctly identified. "Since most treatments that we have been talking about today are not one thing but a bundle of things, the problem of trying to sort out which of the things in the bundle, including things that you might not even have intended to put into the bundle but are just incidental features of the bundle, are the actual ingredients that produce the effect is the problem of sorting out construct validity of cause," said Hedges. Randomized experiments can help sort out these factors, but they don't necessarily protect against misattributing cause. For example, people who know they are in a control group may try harder just because they are in a control group. Or a control group may be demoralized by having been denied something that they thought was valuable.

Different study designs have different strengths, Hedges pointed out. For example, observational studies that take advantage of naturally occurring variation can be subject to confounding variables that threaten their internal validity. Researchers can try to control for this, but, as Hedges pointed out, "how can you know that you controlled for all of the possible confounding variables?"

In contrast, a randomized experiment can control for confounders that even the researchers haven't identified. "So the big strength of randomized experiments is that they have high internal validity," said Hedges. "Their big weakness is they are usually only performable. . . with oddly selected samples that make it somewhat more difficult to claim that there is ready generalizability." Similarly, ethnographic designs can offer insight about known mechanisms, uncover new mechanisms, and test many hypotheses in a single investigation. But sometimes their internal validity is not high, and they can be difficult to generalize since they often involve small and unusual samples.

"No research design is perfect," Hedges said. "You need to know that yourself. [And] if you are planning to get funding for your research, it is probably wise to admit it to others as well. Reviewers and other sophisticated critics know that no design is perfect, and their question to you in evaluating your design is usually whether you know it is imperfect and [whether] you have a strategy for dealing with the imperfections, like a series of studies that each have somewhat different flaws."

Hedges also discussed the pros and cons of using research design consultants. No one person is likely to have all of the skills needed to develop an optimal research design, so a team could involve a research design consultant. "I have been in that role quite a few times in my life, and I would argue that people who do that kind of thing can be helpful," said Hedges. "But based on my own experience with this, and the experience of others who have played this role, you have to be involved early in the planning and research project to be most helpful. The worst thing in the world you can do is hire a very good person or engage a very good person to join you so late in the project that he or she can't really help you very much in planning the design and thinking through various aspects of the project." Similarly, research design consultants have to be able to learn a lot about a research project to be helpful, even though they will never know as much about the research as the original investigators.

ANALYZING THE DATA

The most important thing about the statistical analysis of data, said Kenneth I. Maton, professor of psychology at the University of Maryland, Baltimore County (UMBC), is that statistical methods need to be built into a research project from the beginning. They need "to flow directly from the research questions that you are asking. That is the number-one rule," Maton said. "The techniques that you apply to analyze your data should be those that are appropriate to answer the questions you are asking."

Maton used as an example the analyses he and his students have conducted using data gathered from research focused on the Meyerhoff Scholarship Program at UMBC, which is a comprehensive program for high-achieving high school students who are interested in pursuing doctoral study in the sciences or engineering and who are interested in the advancement of minorities in science and engineering.[3] Maton's group has developed survey items that assess student experiences in the various program components that could affect outcomes. These components range from formal activities like summer bridge programs, to summer research experiences, to

---

[3] K.I. Maton, F.A. Hrabowski III, and C.L. Schmitt. 2000. African American college students excelling in the sciences: College and postcollege outcomes in the Meyerhoff Scholars Program. *Journal of Research in Science Teaching* 37(7): 629-654.

social interaction with other Meyerhoff students. To reduce these items into a useable scale and relate them to outcomes, he and his colleagues performed what is called a *factor analysis*, which is a form of data reduction. There are several ways of conducting such an analysis, but the ultimate result is to show which subsets of items form groups that are more closely associated with other members of the group and less closely associated with the other factors. For example, major aspects of the Meyerhoff program that include financial support, study groups, the summer bridge program, and the quality of interactions with other students in the program form a cluster. More specific aspects of the program associate on another scale, including students' involvement with the community, cultural activities, and mentoring and advising by Meyerhoff staff. Interestingly, the summer research activities were not closely associated with either set of items, thus constituting a unique and separate aspect of the student experience. In general, "data reduction is one important thing that you want to consider if you are going to be using survey items," said Maton.

Another form of data analysis is to compare the experiences and outcomes of different groups. For example, the Meyerhoff program was originally designed for African Americans, but concern about possible legal challenges led to the program being offered to others as well. One analysis of the program compared the experiences of African Americans with those of other groups, including Asian American and white students, with the hypothesis being that African Americans would have a greater sense of support and belonging from the program since it was designed for them. But the comparison revealed that the groups scored equally on this measure. The technique used in this analysis, which is known as *analysis of variance*, "is a way to look at group differences," said Maton. "[It] allows you to say whether the differences in the mean levels of the groups are great enough, given the amount of variation within each group, so that statistically you would say that, 'probably, the difference is not due to chance.'"

Analysis of variance can be used when the measures are continuous, but in many cases the variables being studied take discrete values, such as whether a student does or does not go on to graduate school, or whether a student graduates or not. For example, Maton's research group has compared the Meyerhoff students to students who were accepted into the program but decided to attend a different institution instead, using categorical outcome variables, such as whether the students graduated in a STEM discipline. Maton's group found that a much higher percentage of the Meyerhoff students graduated after four or five years in a STEM discipline—83 percent—compared with 46 percent who declined the offer. In this case, the researchers used a technique called *chi square analysis* to determine whether this difference is statistically significant. They also were able to look at other possible factors between the two groups of students that might have contributed to this difference besides their experiences in the program, such as differences in grade point averages, parental socioeconomic class, and so on. They then used an *analysis of covariance* to study whether some of these factors might have been confounding variables. (For example, Maton pointed out, analysis of covariance could identify temperature as the confounding variable in a study relating level of ice cream sales to homicide rates, as described by Hedges in an earlier presentation.)

Another important research focus is *predictors of outcome*, which measures whether a given variable contributes to an outcome. Multiple linear regression analysis is used to examine which predictor variables contribute to a continuous outcome, whereas logistic regression analysis is used to examine the relationship between predictor variables and categorical outcomes. For example, a logistic regression analysis showed that African American Meyerhoff students, who had lower average SAT scores, were just as likely to gain entrance into a doctoral program as white and Asian American students. "Even though they come in with lower standardized test scores, they are just as likely to go into a doctoral program as these other students," said Maton. "This is a really good finding for the Meyerhoff program."

Maton also emphasized the importance of bringing in outside experts to the research team. "The major take-home message is . . . if you don't have the expertise yourself, you want to bring in consultants to work with you. [And] you want to make sure they understand your project enough and your goals enough so that they can provide useful and helpful consultation," he said.

In addition, Maton stressed the value of combining quantitative data with qualitative data: "I am a firm believer in combining the two." For one thing, the qualitative data help support the quantitative data. With the Meyerhoff program, the combination "helps me believe that this program is affecting these youth," said Maton. "When we talk to them, when we do focus groups with them, when we do ethnographic observation with them, you can see that there is something going on, that these students are developing an identity as African American [science] students, that they want to go out and do something in the world in terms of STEM. . . . when they talk about the Meyerhoff program, they talk about the fact that they feel supported, that they feel inspired, and that they feel incredibly challenged, but also incredibly supported by the program."

Qualitative data analysis does not consist simply of reading through the transcripts of a set of interviews or focus groups. Through a very labor intensive process, codes are developed to analyze the transcript contents. For example, the codes used in a study of educational interventions might relate to the mention of self-efficacy beliefs, a sense of belonging, mentoring, or the presence of role models. The interviews are analyzed, coded, and rechecked. Themes are developed that connect the codes, including negative cases where researchers scour the data set for counterexamples. Software packages bring power to these analyses, because these packages can systematically pull up material that is coded in particular ways.

"It is an iterative process where you are recording, reworking your codes, reworking your themes," said Maton. "In the ideal world, you share your themes with the participants who took part in the interviews and took part in the focus groups. You get some checks from [them and] others, and you always have multiple people working on the project and providing different perspectives. So you can do it more systematically rather than less systematically, but it should be done in a team effort with multiple people involved and multiple ways to check the data."

4

Developing a Research Agenda

Underrepresented minorities—and all students—must navigate a series of experiences in the process of selecting career paths; a research agenda designed to understand which factors influence those decisions also will be complex. In such a circumstance, said National Institutes of Health (NIH) director Elias A. Zerhouni in his keynote address, conclusions should be based on evidence and experimentation, not on belief. "Can you define a testable hypothesis for which you can perform an experiment?" Zerhouni asked. "Step one in making progress is realizing that we need, as a group, to come together with some testable pilots and identify the true drivers without being shy about what the issues are."

Zerhouni mentioned several topics that he believes should be part of a research agenda. For example, mentoring is obviously crucial, he said, but what is it about the mentoring relationship that makes a difference? One interesting question, for example, is what the person being mentored brings to the relationship. "There is no such thing as one-way mentoring," Zerhouni said. "Mentoring is a two-way activity between the mentee and the mentor. And I think that training the mentees in how to learn and how to be a mentee is just as important as mentoring."

Mentoring experiences could be more effective, said Yolanda S. George of the American Association for the Advancement of Science (AAAS), if more were known specifically about mentoring in science, technology, engineering, and mathematics (STEM) disciplines.

She suggested that information is needed on cross-gender and cross-racial STEM mentoring and on mentoring of people with disabilities interested in STEM disciplines. George also called for more mentoring research linked to outcomes, such as entry into STEM college majors, time-to-degree at all degree levels, types of college and university degrees earned, entry into STEM graduate majors, entry into STEM careers by sectors, and advancements in the STEM workforce. At a more fundamental level, George suggested asking the question, "What is the purpose of mentoring?" Students may know that they want to be mentored but may have no idea of what kind of mentoring they need or what they want or need from a mentor.

Talking one on one with the students a program is designed to serve is an essential part of developing and assessing these programs. "Many of us design these programs without including the people that we are trying to target, to understand where they are coming from," said Tuajuanda Jordan, senior program officer for science education at the Howard Hughes Medical Institute (HHMI). "We cannot forget the voices of our students when we are trying to define these programs." Sometimes that means talking with people who are quite different than you and "not in your immediate comfort zone," she observed, but that is the only way to learn what their real concerns are.

Another important factor, said Zerhouni, is the timeframe when interventions are most effective. NIH is focused on the world of higher education, but many interventions may be necessary in the pre-college years. The Meyerhoff Scholarship Program at the University of Maryland, Baltimore County, for example, brings promising minority students to the campus when they are in the 10th or 11th grade to show them what they could accomplish through hard work in high school.[1]

Another critical factor, according to Zerhouni, is the socioeconomic status of students. "I have seen terrifically qualified individuals who just could not afford the career in science that you would want them to follow," he said. Should the amount of financial support be the same for all students, or should it be tailored to an individual and his or her needs? Perhaps financial support should be means-tested rather than the same for everyone. "For young, up-and-coming, minority, and underrepresented candidates, those dollar questions have a huge impact on their decision-making process," said Zerhouni. "When you have $100 and that is your last $100 and you are in the lab with people at a different place in the wealth

---

[1] The Meyerhoff Scholarship Program is discussed in more detail in Chapter 3.

curve, it does taint your judgment. . . . I think we need to be sensitive to that. That parameter never shows up as explicitly as I would like to see it expressed."

Less tangible but just as influential are the cultural factors involved in the development of a scientist. As Zerhouni related, "The one thing I learned when I came to Johns Hopkins was that it did not matter how good you were in math or physics or how good your grades were, you knew your success in science was going to depend enormously on your communication skills and your fitting in to the culture of science." To what extent do minority students fit in with predominantly majority groups, and how do subgroups form within research groups? Effective social science research is needed to explore the environment of the scientific laboratory or school, he said.

"There are many different dimensions to these questions, and we have to be honest about the fact that we may not have performed the science on science that we need to perform," Zerhouni said. "Maybe our strategies are belief based rather than fact based. I think we need to be humble again and address that." The research agenda is much larger than can be handled by any one federal agency, said Zerhouni: the mission "is much larger than any one of us."

In pursuing this research, investigators need to be careful not to overlook the important work that has been done in the past. As Carol J. Burger, associate professor in the Center for Interdisciplinary Studies and director of the Science and Gender Equity Program at Virginia Polytechnic Institute and State University, pointed out, "There is already a community of scholars who have been working on this problem of underrepresentation of minorities and women in STEM for many, many years. There is a rich and deep literature. As my major professor in immunology used to tell me: 'read, read, read, read, read.'"

An additional challenge for pursuing this kind of research is the question of how to maintain the privacy of their students as research subjects despite the fact that researchers often are studying very small numbers of students. AAAS's Daryl E. Chubin suggested that ways might be found to anonymize some of the data yet still be able to extract information from them, perhaps by employing an outside contractor. "It seems to me that somebody on the outside [of funding agencies] has got to be able to do it," said Chubin. "[This approach] may not be as cost effective, but at least we would get the benefit of it."

At the workshop, several points of intervention and stakeholder opportunity were raised. As Howard H. Garrison, planning committee member and deputy executive director for policy and director of the Office of Public Affairs at the Federation of American Societies for Experimental Biology (FASEB), said in introducing the final panel, "every stage matters. We can always point to the person on the other side of us, before us, or after us and say, 'if they were doing a better job, my life would be a lot easier. We would have more students, better students; we would have more professors'. . . . All of us, no matter where we are working, whether it is elementary school, high school, college, graduate school or in professional associations, I think there are things that we can do." The remainder of this chapter summarizes the comments made at the workshop related to different possible points of interventions and stakeholders. A final section addresses the development of a research community dedicated to answering these questions.

PRE-COLLEGE EDUCATION

Because students experience K-12 education first, many proposals to increase the representations of underrepresented minorities in science focus on that level. Interventions at the K-12 level need to start early, said Nicole Crane of Cabrillo College. "We have to go have dinner with mom and dad and the younger kids," she said. "The issues go way back in recruitment, and that is something that is not as well addressed."

Among the programs that have proven especially successful in recruiting and retaining minorities in the sciences, said Howard University's Orlando L. Taylor, are magnet programs in science, technology, and mathematics. "There are many [minority students] who never envisioned themselves doing research, but who get that experience [in magnet schools]. Not all of them will go in that direction, but [these schools] have one of the highest percentages of students who go on to get PhDs and who pursue research careers," said Taylor.

Workshop participants described other programs that have been especially successful. For example, the Institute of Leadership Excellence and Academic Development (I-LEAD) at the Bank Street College of Education in New York City is working with six Catholic schools in the Bronx and Harlem to identify students from low-income, underserved neighborhoods and steer them toward highly selective colleges and universities instead of less selective institutions. "The program has been extremely successful in taking students from fairly moderate aspirations to really high aspirations," Michael T. Nettles of Educational Testing Service said. In the class of 2006, all participating students applied to selective colleges and universities, 91 percent were accepted, and 72 percent enrolled, compared with just 35 percent of a comparable set of students who did not participate in the program. Similarly, in the New York Metro Region Leadership Academy established by Prep for Prep, nearly all of the participating students apply to selective colleges and universities, and most attend. "Before this program existed, these students were underrepresented in rigorous curricula in high school and less likely to take [Advanced Placement] courses," Nettles said. "Now they are more likely to take them."

Nicholas Ingoglia, associate dean of the Graduate School of Biomedical Sciences at the University of Medicine and Dentistry of New Jersey (UMDNJ) Newark campus, pointed out that many students from underprivileged backgrounds may not have much context for what scientific research even entails. "They don't even know what research is; they don't know anything. They are bright kids, but they just don't have the information," he said. The program he described at UMDNJ brings students into the lab and gives them the kind of hands-on experience they were lacking.

Nettles argued that the talent pool of students from minority groups underrepresented in the sciences is much larger than most people realize. The challenge is to get these students to aim high. "Setting the goal to do well, go higher, is very often half the battle," he said.

An especially effective way to do that, several workshop participants said, is through mentoring from students just a few years older than the protégés. According to Robert W. Lent of the University of Maryland, College Park, "exposing students to folks who look like them and are just a little bit older and who have coped with the same environmental obstacles that the younger students are now facing can be extraordinarily helpful—perhaps, in part, for reasons of neutralizing stereotype threat, of normalizing the experience, of saying, 'hey, you deserve to be here.'"

LaRuth C. McAfee, executive director for education at the Center for Layered Polymeric Systems at Case Western Reserve University, described the Polymers Envoys programs, in which high school students from Cleveland public schools do research in university labs. In addition to participating in academic research, these students develop demonstrations that they can take into middle school classrooms "to also get [the middle school] kids more excited, and see that their peers, students who were in their place three years ago, are doing this research, and they are successful in these opportunities," she said.

One important challenge of these programs is that the desired outcomes will likely be many years down the road. As Ingoglia said, "I don't know if any funding agency is going to want to put money into something that is ten years down the line. I think it is a huge problem."

UNDERGRADUATE EDUCATION

Workshop participants highlighted several programs at the undergraduate level in addition to the Meyerhoff Scholarship Program at the University of Maryland, Baltimore County, discussed above. They include the Biology Undergraduate Scholars Program at the University of California, Davis; programs supported by private organizations such as HHMI and the Alfred P. Sloan Foundation; and programs supported by federal agencies, including the National Science Foundation (NSF) and NIH. These programs exhibit great diversity, which is part of their strength. According to Wanda E. Ward, deputy assistant director for social, behavioral, and economic sciences at NSF, the broad portfolio of programs sponsored by NSF "allows us to connect a multiplicity of efforts from a wide-ranging group of experts who can provide insight from various perspectives." However, many of the successful programs tend to be relatively small and expensive, Boston College's David R. Burgess pointed out, partly because they are comprehensive. "Don't create another program—clone these," he said. "But the resources are substantial." However, other workshop participants cautioned against trying to fit a program that works in one setting into another.

According to several workshop participants and speakers, a major problem with existing programs is that they tend not to be institutionalized. Institutions are "unwilling to institutionally support these programs," said Burgess, "usually because the programs are not a departmental program, and departments have the power." As a result, these programs can be susceptible to changing priorities and to affirmative action challenges. When programs are supported with "soft money," said Chubin, they "won't be readily sustained, which means that they will only benefit those cohorts of students who happen to be at the right place at the right time. We obviously have to do better than that."

An interesting question that reflects on the efficacy of existing programs is where underrepresented minorities earn their degrees. An analysis conducted by Burgess and his colleagues has shown that African Americans tend to earn baccalaureate degrees in biology primarily at historically black colleges and universities (HBCUs) and at research II and comprehensive universities, rather than at research I universities.[2] Hispanics earn their biology degrees at a large and diverse group of mostly public research I universities, while American Indians earn their undergraduate biology degrees predominantly at non-research state universities and at smaller and comprehensive colleges. "In all cases," Burgess observed, "it turns out that the minority populations are attending schools and earning their biology degrees in regions of the highest population densities in our country for their communities, which shouldn't be a surprise."

When Burgess looked at where minorities earn doctoral degrees in biology, he noticed an interesting contrast: "It turns out that 13 of the top producers of Hispanic baccalaureates appear in the top 20 list of Hispanic doctoral-granting institutions. However, only 8 of the 20 top producers of biology black biomedical baccalaureates appear in the top 20." Further, Hispanics are earning their biology doctorates at top research universities while African Americans are earning their biology doctorates at research II institutions.

Programs to increase the number of underrepresented minorities who hold faculty positions at top research institutions would be better informed by data on where practicing researchers obtained their degrees, Burgess suggested. For example, he would like to know where the biology faculty at research I universities earned their bachelor's degrees, where they earned their doctorates, and where they did their postdoctoral work. "Early analysis says that the faculty in biology at the top 50 funded departments get their bachelor's and PhDs at highly selective private universities, and at [public] research I universities," said Burgess, but more detailed information might suggest routes that minorities could follow to faculty positions at leading universities.

Several speakers pointed out the value of involving students in research as undergraduates. Taylor, for one, felt that colleges and universities still "have too few minorities engaged in undergraduate research." Much still needs to be learned about the most effective ways to structure those research experiences. For example, Nettles reminded the group that research can be inaccessible to stu-

---

[2]"Research I," "Research II," and "Comprehensive" are categories that were used in previous versions of the Carnegie Classification of Institutions of Higher Education. Although the Carnegie Classification has developed more specific categorizations since 2000, these terms continue to be used colloquially; for example, "research I" generally refers to the nation's most prominent research institutions. See <http://www.carnegiefoundation.org/classifications/> for more information and the current classifications and descriptions.

dents without adequate outside resources: "Some people can't, for example, afford not to work. If we really want to develop the talent among poor people who really need the income, the program has to include some compensation for their time."

Karen Kashmanian Oates, a member of the planning committee and provost and professor of biochemistry at Harrisburg University of Science and Technology, reminded participants to consider the curriculum as well as research experiences. She encouraged the inclusion of "researchable questions that are based on curriculum, and how we are interacting with our students—what is their best learning style. We know so much more now than we did ten years ago about how people learn, but as scientists we haven't changed the way we approach our teaching." One of the breakout discussions suggested looking at measures of student learning as well as qualities that are more difficult to measure, such as motivation, persistence, and problem-solving ability. In reporting back on that session, Chubin asked if these are qualities that can be taught or instilled in students.

Much is still unknown about the extent to which undergraduate research is effective in steering undergraduates toward graduate school and research careers, several workshop participants pointed out. "If we really understand what is going on, . . . we will have a much better understanding about how to improve those programs or practices, or which elements of them could be extracted at a much lower cost," said Carol B. Muller, planning committee member and the founder, president, and chief executive officer of MentorNet. After all, many very productive scientists never engaged in research as undergraduates. What were the experiences that caused them eventually to become researchers?

George pointed out that many students attend multiple institutions and take varying lengths of time to earn their degrees. These pathways should be tracked more effectively, she said, as should the factors that cause pathways to differ. According to Michael Leibowitz, professor and associate dean at UMDNJ's Robert Wood Johnson Medical School, tracking students requires "hard work and creativity and considerable expense, but these things are not impossible. If we reward the successful programs and attempt to disseminate their techniques, I think a lot can be done."

Shirley M. Malcom, the director of education and human resources programs at AAAS, suggested looking beyond the gates of the campus. "Most of the time, when people raise the issue of undergraduate research, they only look to those sets of institution-based experiences, as opposed to looking out into the larger community to see where there may be opportunities in the local crime lab, at the police station, or in an agricultural agency," she said. Malcom noted that another important form of research that young scientists can do is in the policy arena, so that these individuals will be ready to assume policy roles later in their careers.

GRADUATE EDUCATION AND POSTDOCTORAL TRAINING

The social networks for minorities doing research are critical, perhaps especially at the graduate and postdoctoral level. Jordan talked about being the only African American researcher in a research group. But "at night, when I went to the graduate house, there were many more people who looked like me," she said. "It can't be just one person trying to do it all." McAfee described an activity where the Black Graduate Student Association at her graduate institution established a weekly research discussion: "Everyone sets goals for the next week, everyone gives a quick update on what they have been doing for the past week. So that is also a way where they are still being able to interact with other black grad students, but they are also still helping to achieve their ultimate goal of graduation."

One pressing question that remains unanswered is why minorities underrepresented in the sciences do not achieve the same record of research productivity in graduate school as non-minority students and may not participate in as much high-impact research. As Gilda Barabino, professor of biomedical engineering at the Georgia Institute of Technology, said, "even if you are in a research I institution, [publication] numbers are extremely low. Many times, the reason for that is because you are not getting included in modern collaborations, you are not part of the hot project. There is just a multitude of reasons."

Nettles speculated that few minority students experience a "halo effect," where particular students may be selected for achievement and ushered through the graduate school processes, with specific projects, deliverables, deadlines, and support. Taylor agreed: "There is kind of an anointing process in many research environments for graduate students. Students know who the PI or who the lab director's . . . special persons [are]. Once anointed, it makes a big difference in terms of who gets into certain activities: who is asked to go to a meeting, who hangs out and comes to the home for dinner, and so forth. Those things begin those informal, invisible factors that contribute greatly to the research career."

In part, the selection of favored students reflects a model of graduate training rooted in traditional educational structures. But that model may be outmoded, said Walter (Skip) Bollenbacher, professor emeritus at the University of North Carolina at Chapel Hill and vice president of Integrated Learning Innovations: "We have trained scientists the same since we built the university research enterprise—about the same time Sputnik went up. It has occurred during all this time of sophisticated science and complex interdisciplinary work." The graduate students most eagerly sought by employers today, Bollenbacher said, are the ones who know how to organize and work in teams and communicate effectively. "We are training in the 20th-century model, but we live in a 21st-century society."

Several workshop participants warned against painting graduate education with too broad a brush. Different disciplines have quite different approaches—some are characterized by teams, others by individual researchers, some have close ties to industry, others do not. Taylor speculated that differences such as these may even account for why there are more minorities in the humanities, education, and the social sciences than in the life sciences and engineering. Northwestern University's Rick McGee observed that the prospects for employment following graduate school are quite different for different disciplines. An engineer may have good job offers, whereas a PhD in molecular biology faces quite a different set of opportunities and challenges. "We have to stop talking about research careers" in general, said McGee. We have to make "our questions and our terminology more precise than we have in the past."

The issue of employment following graduate school raised the question of graduate education's goals: How should "success" be defined for a graduate student? Simeon Slovacek, a professor at California State University, Los Angeles, noted that he has a very difficult time hiring minority teachers at the charter schools he has helped organize. Success, he said, should include preparing a minority student to be a teacher, not just to get a research grant. What's needed, he said, is "a better and broader definition of what it is we are considering success in the work that we do in preparing science educators." Martin M. Chemers, of the University of California, Santa Cruz, made a similar point: "I think we should expand what outcomes we think are success," he said. "A full-bore attack on the problems we are talking about means [preparing] better high school science teachers, it means putting . . . minority doctors in the community so that if a kid goes to the doctor he can aspire to a medical career. We have to change the whole substrate of society in this area."

It is not possible, as Anthony L. DePass of Long Island

University–Brooklyn pointed out, for every graduate student to become a researcher. "In our looking at what we are trying to improve, we also need to look at exactly what we consider a successful research career. The numbers alone would dictate that we all cannot be at research I institutions. [Other] career tracks are research-related, and we need to consider those as we move on and decide what other measures of success are."

Redefining success also may help ease one of the most intractable problems of graduate education: the stresses apparent in many research environments that make many students, including minorities, turn away from research as a career. Bollenbacher said that he received his first R01 grant[3] from the NIH when he was 30. Today's beginning researchers receive their first R01 grant when they are in their 40s. The funding rate for grant applications is below 20 percent, and, because of budget pressures, even successful applicants are only getting 85 to 90 percent of what they expect, claims Bollenbacher. Such a life can be "brutal," he said. Researchers need to "lobby more to make this a better life, to make it a life where the PI doesn't work 15 hours a day, seven days a week, and the graduate students and the postdocs watch this and say, 'No way, I am not going to do this.'"

Alyson Reed, executive director of the National Postdoctoral Association (NPA), asked about the appeal of a research career. Are these jobs really appealing given the alternatives, she asked. Nettles similarly asked what impression the average student gets of research. "When you have a detailed conversation" about research with students, said Nettles, "they see what your life is like, and they don't necessarily want to emulate it: the kind of work, the kind of time, the concentration." Added Jordan, "just because you are a scientist does not mean you are not a human. There are certain aspects of your life that we must pay attention to." Chubin noted that minorities, in particular, often want to give back to their communities and will be less likely to pursue research if a career in science seems to close off this option. "There are alternatives that will allow them to have work-life balance, and that will be more lucrative and will allow them to fulfill themselves as whole people," he said.

Questions were also raised about whether graduate training is meeting its objectives or if it is offloading some of its components to require more lengthy postdoctoral appointments. "Do we have adequate research training at the PhD?" asked Taylor. "Or have we

---

[3]R01 is the traditional investigator-initiated research project grant offered by the NIH.

piled up too many courses and credits such that, when individuals finish the doctorate, they are really not prepared for the world of work, can't work in teams, [and] have had inadequate experience across disciplinary boundaries, so that they now have to go into a postdoctoral experience to get prepared for a research career?" In fact, one of the breakout discussions suggested that there might be researchable questions related to the development of postdocs and faculty or to identify the characteristics of faculty that might contribute to graduate student attrition.

A different model would be to hire people into what Taylor termed pre-faculty appointments. A PhD recipient could receive the additional research training that the PhD did not provide as a pre-faculty member, but the tenure clock would not start. Young researchers could start their careers, and after about three years they could begin pursuing tenure. "If you start off with the presupposition that you will not hire people without a postdoc, and if you don't have some intervention in terms of the way you take care of your hiring, then you will have little opportunity to change the picture," said Taylor.

Changes in hiring practices require a visible commitment from administrators. "There has to be some kind of institutional leadership by those of us in professional scientific societies and at institutions in terms of the hiring strategy for research I faculty," said Burgess. He believes faculty members have a tendency to hire people who are like themselves. If minority students feel that they would not be comfortable or fit in at a research I university, they may not want to become faculty there, saying "we need to somehow have some leadership at our institutions to break this down."

Malcom pointed out that existing laws and policies can be a spur to fairer hiring practices. "We still have laws on the books, for example, that say we are supposed to bring a diverse pool into a faculty hire," she said. "That is not something that a scientific community can do. It can adjust the behavior that says that if you have a whole lot of diverse students and no diverse faculty, that there is a problem with that. But in terms of affecting the behavior of who is in that pool and allowing or not allowing a hire, if you haven't presented a diverse pool, that is an institutional responsibility. It is related to laws that are not being carried out."

Muller, however, issued a caution about the ability of colleges and universities to make profound changes. "Deans and vice presidents and provosts and presidents aren't necessarily at liberty to make grand sweeping changes," she said. "It is shared governance, but it is more than that. The allegiance of the individual researcher is often much more to his or her discipline and professional connection, not just a single professional society, but to a professional connection of colleagues and work and reputation and publishing and so on and so forth, that goes way beyond whatever the institution can hope to offer up. So we really need to be thinking much more broadly about how we deal with the basics of bias, intentional and otherwise, . . . that we all know and have experienced and witnessed for years, but that needs to be addressed more broadly in the communities in which we work."

To make substantial changes in the lives of minorities both when they are undergraduates and graduates, institutions need to go through a process of "transformation," said several of the workshop participants. Some of the elements of this transformation will be similar at any institution. According to Jordan, "as you talk about institutional transformation, it is very important that we realize that there is no cookie cutter for the primarily white institutions and not for the HBCUs as well. There are some institutional problems that you will find in an HBCU that will also be at a research I institution." This process of transformation has to involve administrators as well as faculty: "It is not just about the faculty designing programs for these target groups. It has to be a community effort that involves the entire institution." And the transformation process itself has to be monitored using good indicators of change.

FUNDERS

Federal agencies, nonprofit organizations, professional societies, and other funders of research can contribute to an understanding of educational interventions in several ways. They can conduct research on their own or support others to do research. They can examine intervention programs that they have funded or look at larger sets of interventions that may affect a discipline or field of science. They can provide incentives for others to conduct research or offer ways to disseminate the results of research—such as through professional journals or other publications.

Reporting on a breakout discussion, NPA's Reed suggested that professional societies and other nonprofit organizations can collaborate with each other to establish a coordinated research agenda and common tools for research. For example, many professional societies support similar interventions, such as travel award programs, fellowship programs, mentoring interactions at meetings, and so on. Reed reported that the breakout group felt that a unified way of studying these interventions could produce valuable information.

Institutions—and especially professional societies—can reflect the importance of this issue through their leadership structure, governance, speaking agendas, invitees to meetings, and other policies. Reed reported that the breakout conversation on these issues went beyond minority affairs committees, fellowship programs, or travel awards: "The interventions should not necessarily be compartmentalized off to the side somewhere; . . . societies need to think holistically about changing their practices," she said.

Federal agencies have devoted attention to these issues and continue to refine their programs. For example, NSF supports the Louis Stokes Alliance for Minority Participation (LSAMP). As Ward explained, LSAMP is built on a dual model of academic integration and disciplinary socialization. An independent evaluation by the Urban Institute showed that underrepresented minorities participating in the program were just as likely to pursue further course work in STEM as non-minority students.[4] The LSAMP is connected to many others at NSF and will now provide support for educational research projects on the baccalaureate attainment of underrepresented minorities.

Jordan also pointed out the contributions that private philanthropies can make: "One of the things that I can do by directing the science education center at Howard Hughes is to engage people in these types of discussions to come there and have these kinds of interactions." In this way, she said, HHMI can "partner with not just NIH, but also with NSF and the Sloan Foundation, and then with individuals out there in the field who are doing these kinds of things, and see if we can't move this effort forward on a more national level."

BUILDING THE RESEARCH COMMUNITY

Educational institutions are not very good at learning from each other, said Chubin. "We don't transfer very much from one setting to another because we think that our student population is unique, our strengths are unique, our constraints are unique, and that everything has to be home grown. That is not very efficient. It is not very smart. A community could overcome that—it could share a lot more than what we are currently sharing."

---

[4] B.C. Clewell, C. Consentino de Cohen, L. Tsui, L. Forcier, E. Gao, N. Young, N. Deterding, and C. West. 2005. *Evaluation of the National Science Foundation Louis Stokes Alliances for Minority Participation Program*. The Urban Institute, Washington, D.C. <http://www.urban.org/publications/411301.html>

One objective of the workshop was to foster the development of a community of scholars interested in pursuing research related to the involvement of minorities in biomedical and behavioral research. In a final session, participants discussed ways to extend that support beyond the meeting itself. One important emphasis was the dissemination of funding opportunities, ongoing projects, and research results. For example, as editor of the *Journal of Women and Minorities in Science and Engineering*, Burger encouraged participants both to read the journal and to submit articles to it. She also emphasized the importance of publishing negative results: why students do not like a project, or why it proved to be difficult to work with a school. Jordan mentioned additional outlets for publication, including *CBE—Life Sciences Education*, a collaboration between AAAS and HHMI that results in a monthly forum on science education in the pages of *Science*, and a similar effort in *Nature*.

Dissemination opportunities also extend well beyond the printed page. An electronic mailing list of past and current awardees from programs that support research into educational interventions would be a way for the community to exchange information. A website on the topic could provide a way to access conference proceedings, abstracts from annual meetings, and other electronic publications. Such a website could provide "a critical review of the literature . . . for those of us who are not experts in those areas," said Clifton A. Poodry of NIH's Division of Minority Opportunities in Research, along with what Rutgers University's Barry R. Komisaruk termed a toolbox of data analysis tools.

A challenge, said Muller, is "how can we use the technology available to us to connect us in new and useful ways—not an overload, not more e-mail than you can deal with, not more listserves than you can deal with—but to help you connect with a group of people who are doing the things that are of most interest to you." In that regard, Burger highlighted the importance of exploring new ways of interaction among students, such as Facebook. "I'll speak for myself," she said, "but I am so far away from that generation that what I think intuitively is worth nothing when it comes to organizing programs for children and for students. So I think we need to share that information with each other."

Conferences also provide an important venue for disseminating information and results. McAfee described a postdoctoral fellowship she did at Stonybrook University supported by the National Academy of Engineering's Center for the Advancement of Scholarship on Engineering Education (CASEE). She conducted research on the experiences of graduate students in STEM disciplines using an interdisciplinary team that combined the expertise of natural and social scientists. McAfee made use of conferences on engineering education, as well as a Gordon Conference on science and technology policy, to discuss her results. But instead of submitting her presentation to the minority affairs division of the conference, she tried to reach those interested in graduate school more generally, who approached the meeting from a broad perspective. She also mentioned connections that have come about by opportunities such as CASEE's annual meeting, as well as networks of those engaged in engineering education. Along similar lines, HHMI and NIH, along with Harvard University, the University of Louisiana at Monroe, and the University of Washington, convened a series of conversations on diversity in the sciences, drawing in both faculty and administrators at regional meetings.[5] A website and publication is being developed by the HHMI organizers to compile best practices and summarize those discussions.

McAfee suggested that such venues can help increase the visibility of these issues and help promote them as valid areas for investigation. Interdisciplinary teams that are formed will not only lead to more effective research projects, but also greater opportunities for publication and dissemination. McAfee also encouraged making use of existing networks; for example, she used the Science Diversity Center in her research, which was established as a place to identify minority-serving institutions that have received federal funding and serves as way to locate institutions with particular facilities and programs.[6]

According to Taylor, "Many of us . . . have come together many times over many years to raise questions like this. We all want to do this, but we haven't done it." So what is different this time? He identified the fact that the researchers who study interventions have recognized the essential need for much greater coordination and communication. "We haven't been able to get our performance together," he said.

Participants acknowledged that the workshop had been a valuable first step. The workshop was not just "a one-day meeting that everybody feels good about and goes home afterward," said FASEB's Garrison. Rather, the workshop began "establishing a community that can help carry this work forward."

---

[5] http://www.hhmi.org/resources/diversity/; http://www.williams.edu/biology/divsciences/

[6] http://sciencediversitycenter.org/

Appendix A

Statement of Task

The study and identification of contributing factors and practices that determine the effectiveness of interventions aimed at increasing the participation of underrepresented minorities in the biomedical and behavioral sciences is critical for program design and success. The National Academies will organize a public workshop that, among its goals, will include the following:

1. An examination of the current state of research related to interventions that influence the participation of underrepresented minorities in biomedical and behavioral sciences and other science, technology, engineering, and mathematics disciplines. This will include an assessment of factors relevant to studies in related disciplines such as psychology, sociology, and economics.

2. The development of research questions that reflect contributions of various factors influencing outcomes. This would include the relationship of these factors to interdisciplinary approaches for scholarly work in the study of interventions that impact the participation of underrepresented minorities in the biomedical and behavioral sciences.

3. Technical assistance on implementing effective methodologies for studying interventions that impact the participation of underrepresented minorities in the biomedical and behavioral sciences.

4. The encouragement of an interdisciplinary community of scholars where outlets (e.g., journals, conferences, sponsored pro-

grams) for scholarly work and discourse are identified relevant to this area of study.

This public workshop will feature invited presentations and discussions. An individually authored summary of the workshop will be prepared by a designated rapporteur, who will not be a member of the ad hoc committee that will plan and conduct the event.

Appendix B

Workshop Information

UNDERSTANDING INTERVENTIONS THAT ENCOURAGE MINORITIES TO
PURSUE RESEARCH CAREERS:
MAJOR QUESTIONS AND APPROPRIATE METHODS

Thursday-Friday, May 3-4, 2007

Auditorium
American Association for the Advancement of Science
1200 New York Avenue, N.W. • Washington, D.C. 20005

AGENDA

THURSDAY, MAY 3, 2007

8:00 a.m.   **Registration opens**

8:30 a.m.   **Welcome and Introductions**
- Anthony L. DePass (Committee Co-Chair), *Associate Dean of Research and Associate Professor of Biology, Long Island University–Brooklyn*
- Larry V. Hedges (Committee Co-Chair), *Board of Trustees Professor of Statistics and Social Policy, Northwestern University*

8:45 a.m.   **Sponsor's Charge to Workshop Participants**
- Clifton A. Poodry, *Director, Division of Minority Opportunities in Research, National Institute of General Medical Sciences, NIH*

9:00 a.m.	**Setting the Context: Factors Affecting Career Choice and Training** This session will look at the underlying issues of career choice from the perspective of different disciplines, such as psychology, higher education studies, and economics. The session will emphasize the systems aspect of students' decision-making process, the way that many different factors contribute, and highlight different approaches to these questions. Session Chair: Carol B. Muller (Committee Member), *Founder, President, and Chief Executive Officer, MentorNet*<ul><li>Robert W. Lent, *Professor of Counseling and Personnel Services and Co-Director, Counseling Psychology Program, College of Education, University of Maryland, College Park*</li><li>Claude Steele, *Director, Center for Advanced Study in the Behavioral Sciences; Professor of Psychology and Lucie Stern Professor in the Social Sciences, Stanford University*</li><li>Michael T. Nettles, *Senior Vice President and Edmund W. Gordon Chair of the Policy Evaluation and Research Center, Educational Testing Service*</li><li>Anne Preston, *Associate Professor of Economics, Haverford College*</li></ul>
10:45 a.m.	Break
11:10 a.m.	**Setting the Context: Responses and Discussion** Session Chair: Karen Kashmanian Oates (Committee Member), *Provost and Professor of Biochemistry, Harrisburg University of Science and Technology*<ul><li>Orlando L. Taylor, *Vice Provost for Research, Dean of the Graduate School, and Professor of Communication, Howard University*</li></ul>
12:00 p.m.	Lunch
1:00 p.m.	**Remarks from NIGMS Director**<ul><li>Jeremy M. Berg, *Director, National Institute of General Medical Sciences, NIH*</li></ul>

1:15 p.m.   **Keynote Address**
- Elias A. Zerhouni, *Director, National Institutes of Health*

1:45 p.m.   **State of Knowledge and Avenues of Investigation**
This session will provide an overview of the existing knowledge base and introduce some of the questions and approaches that are currently being pursued.

Session Chair: Daryl E. Chubin (Committee Member), *Director, AAAS Center for Advancing Science & Engineering Capacity, American Association for the Advancement of Science*
- David R. Burgess, *Professor of Biology, Boston College*
- Yolanda S. George, *Deputy Director, Education and Human Resources Programs, American Association for the Advancement of Science*

2:50 p.m.   Break

3:10 p.m.   **Technical Assistance Workshop**
This session will focus on technical aspects of research in this area, with discussion of issues such as framing of researchable questions, experimental design, and quantitative analysis.

Session Chair: Larry V. Hedges (Committee Co-Chair), *Board of Trustees Professor of Statistics and Social Policy, Northwestern University*

Overview of NIH Efficacy of Interventions to Promote Research Careers R01 Program
- Shiva P. Singh, *Program Director, Division of Minority Opportunities in Research, National Institute of General Medical Sciences, NIH*

1. Problem Formulation: Asking answerable questions that will advance our understanding of how to increase minority representation in biomedical and behavioral sciences.

This includes situating the research questions in the context of some body of existing knowledge (theory or empirical work). It also involves posing questions that relate to what is known and promises to advance it in a meaningful way. It requires research questions that are broad enough to be important but narrow enough to be answered (or informed in a meaningful way) from a feasible research study. This discussion will be grounded in the kinds of research problems that are relevant to understanding how to increase minority representation in biomedical and behavioral sciences.

- Barry R. Komisaruk, *Associate Dean of the Graduate School, Professor II of Psychology, and Rutgers University Board of Governors Distinguished Service Professor, Rutgers, The State University of New Jersey*
- Martin M. Chemers, *Professor of Psychology, University of California, Santa Cruz*

2. Research Design: Specifying procedures to collect data that can inform that question.

This begins with making clear what will be done (what the research design is). It will include providing a persuasive argument that the proposed research design is feasible (e.g., that it can be carried out, that the individuals invited are likely to participate in the study, etc.), and that the proposed design can provide clear answers to the research questions. At a minimum, this requires a persuasive argument that the proposed design minimizes possible biases and that the proposed analyses will have enough precision or statistical power to detect the effects or relations between variables that are crucial to answering the research questions. It also includes descriptions of how key research concepts used (such as interventions and measures of outcomes) will be operationalized.

- Larry V. Hedges (Committee Co-Chair), *Board of Trustees Professor of Statistics and Social Policy, Northwestern University*

3. Analysis: Specifying the procedure that will be used to reach conclusions from the data collected.

This includes specifying a data reduction and/or analysis procedure that is appropriate for the research design and will provide clear answers to the research questions. The session will not provide an exhaustive discussion of all relevant analysis procedures but will provide examples of some of the most relevant techniques—and motivate why they should be considered.
- Kenneth I. Maton, *Professor of Psychology, University of Maryland, Baltimore County*

5:30 p.m.　Reception and informal discussion
Sponsored by the Howard Hughes Medical Institute

FRIDAY, MAY 4, 2007

8:00 a.m.　**Breakout discussions on research questions and approaches**

This session will follow on the earlier discussions, allowing participants to interact with other participants from similar types of institutions in smaller groups and focus on the types of research questions and approaches that are of most interest.

Each breakout group should prepare to make a 5-minute presentation on the most important research questions and issues during the 9:30 a.m. reporting back session.

There will be three breakout sessions, based upon institution type:
- Research Institutions: *Auditorium*
- Primarily Undergraduate Institutions: *Abelson/Haskins Conference Room*
- Professional Societies: *Revelle Conference Room*

Others (e.g., government employees) are welcome to attend the session of their choice.

9:30 a.m.   **Reporting back on breakout discussions**
            Moderator: Anthony L. DePass (Committee Co-Chair), *Associate Dean of Research and Associate Professor of Biology, Long Island University–Brooklyn*

10:10 a.m. Break

10:30 a.m. **Panel on next steps, including community building and facilitating advancement**
            This session will focus on the next steps for moving the research agenda forward. Among the panelists will be representatives from those who can help provide a venue for future work and discussion.

            Session Chair: Howard H. Garrison (Committee Member), *Deputy Executive Director for Policy and Director, Office of Public Affairs, Federation of American Societies for Experimental Biology*
            - Carol J. Burger, *Associate Professor, Center for Interdisciplinary Studies, and Director, Science & Gender Equity Program, Virginia Polytechnic Institute and State University; Editor-in-Chief,* Journal of Women and Minorities in Science and Engineering
            - Tuajuanda Jordan, *Senior Program Officer for Science Education, Howard Hughes Medical Institute*
            - LaRuth C. McAfee, *Executive Director for Education, Department of Macromolecular Science and Engineering, Case Western Reserve University*
            - Wanda E. Ward, *Deputy Assistant Director for Social, Behavioral & Economic Sciences (currently on detail as Deputy Assistant Director for Education and Human Resources), National Science Foundation*

12:30 p.m. **Concluding session**
            - Anthony L. DePass (Committee Co-Chair), *Associate Dean of Research and Associate Professor of Biology, Long Island University–Brooklyn*
            - Larry V. Hedges (Committee Co-Chair), *Board of Trustees Professor of Statistics and Social Policy, Northwestern University*

12:45 p.m. Workshop adjourns

APPENDIX B

SPEAKER AND PANELIST BIOGRAPHIES

Jeremy M. Berg became director of the National Institute of General Medical Sciences (NIGMS), one of the National Institutes of Health, in November 2003. He oversees a $1.9 billion budget that funds basic research in the areas of cell biology, biophysics, genetics, developmental biology, pharmacology, physiology, biological chemistry, bioinformatics, and computational biology. The Institute supports more than 4,500 research grants—about 10 percent of the grants funded by NIH as a whole—as well as a substantial amount of research training and programs designed to increase the number of minority biomedical scientists.

Prior to his appointment as NIGMS director, Dr. Berg directed the Institute for Basic Biomedical Sciences at Johns Hopkins University School of Medicine in Baltimore, where he also served as professor and director of the Department of Biophysics and Biophysical Chemistry. In addition, he directed the Markey Center for Macromolecular Structure and Function and co-directed the W.M. Keck Center for the Rational Design of Biologically Active Molecules at the university.

Dr. Berg's research focuses on the structural and functional roles that metal ions, especially zinc, have in proteins. He has made major contributions to understanding how zinc-containing proteins bind to the genetic material DNA or RNA and regulate gene activity. His work, and that of others in the field, has led to the design of metal-containing proteins that control the activity of specific genes. These tailored proteins are valuable tools for basic research on gene function, and such proteins could one day have medical applications in regulating genes involved in diseases, as well. Dr. Berg has also made contributions to our understanding of systems that target proteins to specific compartments within cells and to the use of sequence databases for predicting aspects of protein structure and function.

Dr. Berg served on the faculty at Johns Hopkins from 1986 to 2003. Immediately before his faculty appointment, he was a postdoctoral fellow in biophysics at the university. His honors include a Presidential Young Investigator Award (1988–1993), the American Chemical Society Award in Pure Chemistry (1993), the Eli Lilly Award for Fundamental Research in Biological Chemistry (1995), and the Maryland Outstanding Young Scientist of the Year (1995). He also received teaching awards from both medical students and graduate students and served as an advisor to the Johns Hopkins Postdoctoral Association since its founding.

Dr. Berg received BS and MS degrees in chemistry from Stanford

University in 1980 and a PhD in chemistry from Harvard University in 1985. He is a coauthor of more than 130 research papers and three textbooks, *Principles of Bioinorganic Chemistry, Biochemistry (5th Edition* and *6th Edition)* and *A Clinical Companion to Accompany Biochemistry*. NIGMS supported Dr. Berg's research from 1986 to 2003.

Carol J. Burger is an associate professor in the Department of Interdisciplinary Studies and coordinator of the Science and Gender Equity Program at Virginia Polytechnic Institute and State University (Virginia Tech). She received a BA in chemistry from Dominican University, River Forest, Illinois, and a PhD in cellular immunology from Virginia Tech.

Dr. Burger has been interested in gender equity issues in science for many years. She is the founder and editor of the *Journal of Women and Minorities in Science and Engineering,* now in its 12th year of publication. She served as senior program director, Program for Women and Girls, National Science Foundation in 1996. She teaches introduction to women's studies, biology of women, and women and science classes.

She has been a co-investigator for the NSF-funded projects *Counseling for Gender Equity; Women in Information Technology: Pivotal Transitions from School to Careers;* and *Investigating the Gender Component: Cultures that Promote Equity in Undergraduate Engineering.*

Dr. Burger has authored monographs, over 50 peer-reviewed papers about tumor immunology research and women and STEM, and several book chapters and encyclopedia entries. She is the co-editor of the recently published book *Reconfiguring the Firewall: Recruiting Women to Information Technology across Cultures and Continents.*

David R. Burgess is a professor of biology at Boston College and a past president of the Society for the Advancement of Chicanos and Native Americans in Science, a 30-year-old organization committed to increasing the number of Hispanic and Native American scientists. His Cherokee great grandmother was a medicine woman, his father was a teacher and junior high school principal honored for serving minority students, and his mother was a homemaker. He was raised in New Mexico and Northern California. His current research, funded by the National Institutes of Health since 1977, is in the area of cell division and on the science education pipeline for American Indians. He has received several awards, including a Research Career Development Award from the NIH and the E.E. Just Award from the American Society for Cell Biology, where he was recently elected to Council. He has been elected Fellow of the American Association for the Advancement of Science (AAAS).

Dr. Burgess has served on numerous national panels, both in basic science review and on study sections whose goal is to increase the diversity of scientists. He serves on the Minority Action Committee of the American Society for Cell Biology, as advisor to the National Science Foundation and the AAAS for the NSF Alliance for Graduate Education for the Professoriate program, and on the Committee on Opportunity in Science for AAAS. He has presented keynote addresses and lectures to tribal colleges, scientific societies, universities, and other organizations on his research and in the area of training disparities for minorities in the sciences. Dr. Burgess has served as an advisor to the Indian Health Service/National Institutes of General Medical Sciences, the National Institute on Drug Abuse, and the National Science Foundation and has testified before the Congressional Commission on the Advancement of Women and Minorities in Science, Engineering, and Technology Development. He served as a member of the Advisory Committee for the Office of Research on Minority Health at the NIH, the Advisory Committee to the Director at NIH, the NIH National Human Genome Research Institute Advisory Council, the NSF Committee on Equal Opportunity in Science and Engineering, and the Biological and Environmental Research Advisory Committee for the Department of Energy.

Martin M. Chemers is professor of psychology at the University of California, Santa Cruz. Dr. Chemers arrived at UC Santa Cruz in 1995 to accept an appointment as the dean of social sciences and professor of psychology. At UC Santa Cruz, he also served as interim executive vice-chancellor and provost (December 2003–April 2004) and as acting chancellor (April 2004–February 2005). Prior to his tenure at UC Santa Cruz, he was the Henry R. Kravis Professor of Leadership and Organizational Psychology and director of the Kravis Leadership Institute at Claremont McKenna College. He was previously on the faculties of the Universities of Illinois, Delaware, Washington, and Utah where he was chair of the Department of Psychology.

Since receiving his PhD in social psychology from the University of Illinois in 1968, he has been an active researcher and has published books and articles on leadership, culture and organizational diversity, and academic success and adjustment. His popular, practitioner-oriented book *Improving Leadership Effectiveness: The Leader Match Concept* (written with Fred Fiedler) is widely used as a basis for leadership training. Dr. Chemers' books have been translated into German, Chinese, Japanese, Swedish, Spanish, and Portuguese. His most recent book, *An Integrative Theory of Leadership*, was published in 1997. The Japanese edition was published in 1999.

His current research is focused on psychological factors that affect the academic success and adjustment of underrepresented minority students.

Yolanda S. George is deputy director and program director of the Education and Human Resources Directorate at the American Association for the Advancement of Science (AAAS). Her responsibilities include conceptualizing, developing, implementing, and planning multiyear projects related to increasing the participation of minorities, women, and persons with disabilities in science and engineering. She directs or co-directs a number of projects including Science Linkages in the Community, the AAAS Black Church Project, and Science Education Reform for All (a joint science policy project with the Council of Chief State School Officers). These initiatives are all aimed at developing and strengthening out-of-school programs for school-age children operated by community-based groups including youth-serving organizations, churches, science museums, zoos, libraries, and others.

She has served as director of development for the Association of Science-Technology Centers and director of a pre-college, university retention, and pre-graduate school program at the University of California, Berkeley. As a laboratory biologist, Ms. George worked with a biophysics group involved in cell cycle using the flow cytometer and the cell sorter.

Ms. George has authored or co-authored over 35 papers, pamphlets, and hands-on science manuals including *Get into the Equation: Math and Science, Parents and Children*; the *In Touch with Science* series (a series of six inquiry-based manuals for use with parent youth-serving organizations); and *Science and Mathematics Reform: What Do Parents Need to Know to Get Involved?* She has several service awards from Lawrence Livermore Laboratory and University of California, Berkeley. She also has received local appreciation awards from the New Orleans Mayor's Office and Greater New Orleans Urban League. She received her BS and MS in biology from Xavier University of Louisiana and Clark University in Georgia, respectively.

Larry V. Hedges: See biographical sketch in Appendix C.

Tuajuanda Jordan is senior program officer for science education programs at the Howard Hughes Medical Institute. While earning a BS degree in chemistry from Fisk University in Nashville, Tennessee, she engaged in research focused in organic synthesis as a MARC Scholar under the direction of the late Dr. I. Wesley Elliott. Dr. Jordan earned a PhD in biochemistry from Purdue University in West Lafayette, Indiana, with Dr. Victor Rodwell as a MARC Predoctoral Fellow. She then did postdoctoral work with Dr. Judith Harmony at the University of Cincinnati, Medical Center, in pharmacognosy and cell biophysics.

In 1994, she became a faculty member in the Department of Chemistry at Xavier University of Louisiana in New Orleans, where she advanced to associate professor before assuming the position of associate dean in the College of Arts and Sciences in 2003. In 2005, Dr. Jordan was named associate vice president for academic affairs at Xavier. During her time at Xavier, Dr. Jordan served as program director of the National Science Foundation's Model Institution of Excellence Program. She was also a visiting scholar in the Department of Biophysics at the University of Michigan.

Dr. Jordan has devoted much of her professional career to mentoring students and working with programs designed to retain underrepresented minorities in the STEM disciplines. She is currently a member of the NIH MORE Division's Minority Access to Research Careers subcommittee and has served as the chair of NIH's Minority Biomedical Research Support program and on numerous NIH and NSF scientific review panels.

Barry R. Komisaruk is a behavioral neuroscientist at Rutgers, The State University of New Jersey, serving as Professor II in the Department of Psychology, Rutgers University Board of Governors Distinguished Service Professor, associate dean of the Graduate School, and adjunct professor in the Department of Radiology at University of Medicine and Dentistry of New Jersey. He has recently returned to Rutgers University from a three-year U.S. government service as program director in the MORE Division of the National Institute of General Medical Sciences of the National Institutes of Health. Dr. Komisaruk graduated from the City University of New York with a BS in biology, received his PhD in psychobiology from Rutgers University's campus at Newark, was an NIH postdoctoral fellow in neuroendocrinology at the Brain Research Institute of UCLA, and joined the faculty of Rutgers in 1966.

Dr. Komisaruk has received continuous research funding via numerous research grants and research awards, including those from the NIH, National Science Foundation, Christopher Reeve Paralysis Foundation, and, currently, The New Jersey Commission on Spinal Cord Research. His total grant funding has exceeded $7 million. His area of research specialty is the role of the brain, spinal cord, and peripheral nervous system in the control of reproductive behavior and physiology, and pain control, in humans and laboratory animals. His expertise in research methodology includes human brain imaging using functional magnetic resonance imaging, positron emission tomography, and electrophysiology.

Dr. Komisaruk has served on the Psychobiology Review Panel of the NSF, the editorial boards of biomedical and behavioral journals, and grant review panels of the NIH. He has served as the chairman of the Institutional Review Board for the Protection of Human Subjects in Research at Rutgers University. He has been the doctoral dissertation supervisor of 22 PhD students and primary supervisor of 14 postdoctoral researchers; established a faculty-doctoral student exchange program with five universities and research centers in Mexico, including CINVESTAV (Centro de Investigación y de Estudios Avanzados); and conceptualized and played a major role in the development of the Center for Molecular and Behavioral Neuroscience at Rutgers University. He has published more than 145 research papers, more than 150 conference abstracts, and three books, the most recent of which, coauthored with Carlos Beyer-Flores and Beverly Whipple, is entitled *The Science of Orgasm*, published by the Johns Hopkins University Press in 2006, now in its second printing.

Robert W. Lent is professor and co-director of the Counseling Psychology Program in the Department of Counseling and Personnel Services at the University of Maryland, College Park. He received his PhD in counseling psychology from The Ohio State University in 1979. After serving as staff psychologist at the University of Minnesota's Student Counseling Bureau from 1979 to 1985, he joined the counseling psychology faculty at Michigan State University (1985–1995). He has been at the University of Maryland since 1995. Dr. Lent has published extensively on applications of social cognitive theory to academic and career behavior. His other research interests include counselor training and development, psychological wellness, relationship adjustment processes, and promotion of health behaviors. Dr. Lent is a Fellow of Division 17 (Counseling Psychology) of the American Psychological Association and a recipient of the John L. Holland Award for Outstanding Achievement in Career and Personality Research. Dr. Lent is co-editor, with S.D. Brown, of the *Handbook of Counseling Psychology* (1st–3rd editions) and the newly released text *Career Development and Counseling: Putting Theory and Research to Work*. Along with M.L. Savickas, he has also co-edited *Convergence in Career Development Theories: Implications for Science and Practice*. He serves as associate editor of the *Journal of Social and Clinical Psychology* and is also on the editorial boards of the *Journal of Counseling Psychology* and the *Journal of Vocational Behavior*.

Kenneth I. Maton is professor of psychology and director of the Community-Social Psychology PhD Program in Human Services Psychology at the University of Maryland, Baltimore County. His research focuses primarily on minority student achievement, including longitudinal evaluation of the Meyerhoff Scholars Program at UMBC. Recent books include *Investing in Children, Youth, Families and Communities: Strengths-Based Research and Policy* (edited volume; American Psychological Association) and *Overcoming the Odds: Raising Academically Successful African American Females* (co-author; Oxford University Press). Dr. Maton is past-president of the Society for Community Research and Action (SCRA; APA Division 27), and the most recent winner of SCRA's Distinguished Contribution to Theory and Research Award. He serves on the editorial boards of the *American Journal of Community Psychology*, *Analysis of Social Issues and Public Policy*, and *Journal of Community Psychology*.

LaRuth C. McAfee is executive director for education at the Center for Layered Polymeric Systems (CLiPS), headquartered at Case Western Reserve University in Cleveland, Ohio. CLiPS is a new NSF Science and Technology Center established in August 2006. In her position, Dr. McAfee oversees all education and diversity programs in the Center, which comprises 11 member institutions. These programs include initiatives to encourage pre-college students to pursue polymer science careers, research and course development efforts for undergraduate and graduate students, and a unique research and educational partnership called the Case-Fisk Alliance.

Prior to joining CLiPS, Dr. McAfee completed a postdoctoral research project in engineering education at the Stony Brook University Department of Technology and Society. That project was sponsored by the National Academy of Engineering's Center for the Advancement of Scholarship on Engineering Education. In the position, she studied promising practices in doctoral STEM education, with a special focus on programs to successfully recruit, retain, graduate, and place minority students.

A native of Ann Arbor, Michigan, Dr. McAfee earned her BSE

in chemical engineering at the University of Michigan and her PhD in chemical engineering from the Massachusetts Institute of Technology. At MIT she researched the use of liquid crystalline block copolymers for actuator applications.

Michael T. Nettles is senior vice president for policy evaluation and research and holds the Edmund W. Gordon Chair for Policy Evaluation and Research at Educational Testing Service in Princeton, New Jersey. He has a national reputation as a policy researcher on educational assessment, student performance and achievement, educational equity, and higher education finance. Dr. Nettles' research covers such issues as educational access, opportunity, attainment, the consequences of education for various population groups in the United States, state and national assessment, educational funding policies, and educational testing of students at all levels of education. His publications reflect his broad interest in public policy, student and faculty access, opportunity, achievement, and educational assessment at both the K-12 and post-secondary levels. Dr. Nettles is the co-author of *Three Magic Letters: Getting to Ph.D.*

A native of Nashville, Dr. Nettles received his BA in political science at the University of Tennessee and master's degrees in political science and in higher education and a PhD in higher education from Iowa State University.

Clifton A. Poodry is director of the Division of Minority Opportunities in Research at the National Institute of General Medical Sciences, where he oversees the administration of grants designed to increase the number and capabilities of minority biomedical scientists. These grants support a variety of activities, including research training, infrastructure improvement, curriculum enrichment, and laboratory research at minority institutions. A biologist turned scientific administrator with research expertise in developmental genetics, Dr. Poodry had a 22-year research and teaching career in cell biology and developmental genetics in *Drosophila* at the University of California, Santa Cruz, prior to joining NIH.

Dr. Poodry was a member of the Smithsonian Council from 1997 to 2003. He served as vice-chairperson of the National Research Council's Committee on the High School Biology Curriculum in U.S. Schools (1988–1990) and was a recipient of a National Science Foundation grant to provide training activities to teachers at American Indian schools (1988–1990). He has been a workshop leader for teacher training activities with the American Indian Science and Engineering Society (AISES) since 1990.

Dr. Poodry is a native of the Tonawanda Seneca Indian Reservation in western New York. He has twice been elected to the Board of Directors of the Society for Advancement of Chicanos and Native Americans in Science. He is a former board member of AISES and a 1995 recipient of its highest award, the Ely S. Parker Award, for lifelong accomplishments in science and contributions to the American Indian community. Poodry earned his PhD from Case Western Reserve University and received an honorary doctorate of science from the State University of New York at Buffalo in 1999.

Dr. Poodry has particular interest in science education and issues pertaining to American Indian participation in genetics research. He is the author of over 40 scientific papers and book chapters.

Anne Preston is professor and chair of the Department of Economics at Haverford College and previously taught at Wellesley College and Stony Brook University. She received her BA from Princeton University and her PhD from Harvard University. One of her primary research interests is the economics of the scientific labor force. Dr. Preston's book *Leaving Science* (Russell Sage Foundation, 2004) analyzes occupational exit of scientifically trained men and women with special attention to differences in levels of attrition, reasons for attrition, and consequences of attrition by gender. She is also co-author of *The Competitive Edge—Managing Human Resources in Nonunion and Union Firms*. Dr. Preston was awarded the Drucker Prize for best paper in the journal *Nonprofit Leadership and Management* in 1991 and was a visiting scholar at the Russell Sage Foundation from 1997 to 1998.

Shiva P. Singh is a program director in the Division of Minority Opportunities in Research (MORE) at the National Institute of General Medical Sciences (NIGMS). He manages a portfolio of research and training grants (including MBRS SCORE, RISE, and IMSD, MARC U-STAR, Bridges, Efficacy of Interventions, and K99/R00 grants) in the MORE Division. Prior to this position, Dr. Singh served as a scientific review administrator (SRA), managing the review of research training grants and institutional program project-type applications at NIGMS. As SRA, he organized and managed the panel review of the first cycle of Efficacy of Interventions (R01) applications at NIGMS. Dr. Singh came to NIGMS from Alabama State University (ASU) in Montgomery, where he was professor and chair, Department of Biological Sciences, and director of the university's Biomedical Research and Training Programs.

Dr. Singh earned a BS (with highest honors) in agriculture (1969) and MS in plant pathology and biochemistry (1971), both from Pant University of Agriculture and Technology in India, and a PhD in microbiology (1976) from Auburn University in Alabama. Dr. Singh's research interests at ASU focused on the immunochemical structure of the outer membrane proteins of gram-negative bacteria, the expression of HIV epitopes in *Salmonella*, and genomic fingerprinting of pneumococci. He also directed the training of numerous high school, undergraduate, and graduate students; more than 75 of these students later pursued MD, PhD, or other professional degrees.

Claude Steele is Lucie Stern Professor in the Social Sciences and past chair of the Department of Psychology at Stanford University. He is also the director of the Center for Advanced Study in the Behavioral Sciences. He received his BA from Hiram College and his MA and PhD from The Ohio State University. Steele has received the Dean's Teaching Award at Stanford University, the William James Fellow Award from the American Psychological Society, the Kurt Lewin Award and the Gordon Allport Prize in Social Psychology from the Society for the Psychological Study of Social Issues, the Distinguished Scientific Contribution Award and the Senior Award for Distinguished Contributions to Psychology in the Public Interest from the American Psychological Association, and the Cattell Faculty Fellowship. He is a member of the American Academy of Arts and Sciences and the National Academy of Sciences and he has been awarded honorary doctorates from the University of Michigan, University of Chicago, Yale University, and Princeton University.

Orlando L. Taylor is vice provost for research, dean of the graduate school, and professor of communications at Howard University. Prior to joining the Howard faculty in 1973, Taylor was a faculty member at Indiana University. He also has served as a visiting professor at Stanford University and visiting scholar at the Carnegie Foundation for the Advancement of Teaching.

Dr. Taylor is a national leader in graduate education and within his discipline. He is currently or has served previously as a member of numerous national boards, including the board of directors of the Council of Graduate Schools, for which he served as board chair in 2001. He is also a past president of the Northeastern Association of Graduate Schools and the National Communication Association. He is a former member of the Advisory Committee of the Directorate for Education and Human Resources of the National Science Foundation and of the Advisory Council at the National Institutes of

Health. He is also the former president of the Consortium of Social Science Associations and a current member of the Board of Trustees of the University Corporation for Atmospheric Research. He chairs the National Advisory Board for the Center for the Integration of Research, Teaching and Learning, a major NSF-funded center at the University of Wisconsin.

Currently, Vice Provost Taylor serves as PI on major grants from the National Science Foundation to increase the production of minority PhD recipients in science, technology, mathematics and engineering and in the social, behavioral and economic sciences, as well as from the U.S. Department of Education to develop collaborative academic and research programs between universities in Brazil and in four European Union countries with those in the United States. He is the author of numerous articles, chapters, and books.

Purdue University awarded Vice Provost Taylor an Honorary Doctor of Letters degree in 1994 and Hope College awarded him an Honorary Doctor of Letters degree in August 2001. DePauw University awarded him a Doctor of Pedagogy degree in 2004. The American Speech-Language-Hearing Association awarded him its highest award, Honors of the Association, and the Alumni Association of the University of Michigan awarded him its Distinguished Service Alumni Award. In August 2007, Taylor received the Honorary Degree, Doctor of Higher Education from The Ohio State University.

Dr. Taylor received his bachelor's degree from Hampton University, master's degree from Indiana University, and PhD degree from the University of Michigan.

Wanda E. Ward is deputy assistant director for the Social, Behavioral and Economic (SBE) Sciences Directorate of the National Science Foundation (NSF). She attained her BA in psychology and the Afro-American Studies Certificate from Princeton University in 1976 and her PhD in psychology from Stanford University in 1981.

After 10 years as assistant and associate professor of psychology at the University of Oklahoma, she left academe in 1991 to accept a new position as program director of career access programs with the National Science Foundation (NSF). Dr. Ward moved on to join the Education and Human Resources Directorate at NSF in January 1992, where she held increasing positions of leadership, from program officer to senior associate for policy and planning, and where she played a major role in the development and implementation of the Presidential Awards for Excellence in Science, Mathematics and Engineering Mentoring Program (the nation's highest award for mentoring, established by the White House Office of Science and Technology Policy and administered by NSF).

In 1997 Dr. Ward was appointed assistant to the deputy director in the Office of the Director, serving as principal advisor to the director, deputy director, and various management officials in promoting the goal of a diverse, globally oriented workforce of scientists and engineers and a more scientifically and technologically literate U.S. citizenry. She served as the NSF representative to the Interagency Working Group on the U.S. Science and Technology Workforce of the Future of the President's National Science and Technology Council (NSTC) Committee on Science. She co-chaired that working group's 1998 national workshop on the workforce and managed the publication of the *Proceedings of a Workshop on the U.S. Science, Engineering and Technology Workforce of the Future: National Strategy, National Portfolio, National Resource Base* (1999). In addition, Ward serves as the executive liaison to the Congressionally mandated Committee for Equal Opportunities in Science and Engineering and to the Congressional Commission on the Advancement of Women and Minorities in Science, Engineering and Technology Development.

In her new role as deputy assistant director for SBE, Dr. Ward is the primary assistant to the assistant director in providing leadership and direction to the Directorate for Social, Behavioral, and Economics Sciences

Dr. Ward is a member of the American Psychological Association, where she served as NSF Liaison to the APA Commission on Ethnic Minority Recruitment, Retention and Training in Psychology; the American Association for the Advancement of Science; the Association of Black Psychologists; and the American Educational Research Association.

Elias A. Zerhouni is the director of the National Institutes of Health, where he leads the nation's medical research agency and oversees the NIH's 27 Institutes and Centers with more than 18,000 employees and a fiscal year 2006 budget of $28.6 billion. The NIH investigates the causes, treatments, and preventive strategies for both common and rare diseases helping to lead the way toward important medical discoveries that improve people's health and save lives. More than 83 percent of the NIH's funding is awarded through almost 50,000 competitive grants to more than 325,000 scientists and research support staff at more than 3,000 universities, medical schools, and other research institutions in every state and around the world. About 10 percent of the NIH's budget supports projects conducted by nearly

6,000 scientists in its own laboratories, most of which are on the NIH campus in Bethesda, Maryland.

Dr. Zerhouni, a well-respected leader in the field of radiology and medicine, has spent his career providing clinical, scientific, and administrative leadership. Since being named by President George W. Bush to serve as the 15th director of the National Institutes of Health, beginning in May 2002, Dr. Zerhouni has overseen the completion of the doubling of the NIH budget, initiated the NIH Roadmap for Medical Research, established an NIH-wide research initiative to address the obesity epidemic, supported the NIH Neuroscience Blueprint, supported the reduction of health disparities and barriers to opportunity for minority individuals, ensured public access to NIH-funded research results, committed to earn the public's trust, and enhanced the leadership of NIH.

Prior to joining the NIH, Dr. Zerhouni served as executive vice-dean of Johns Hopkins University School of Medicine, chair of the Russell H. Morgan Department of Radiology and Radiological Science, and Martin Donner Professor of Radiology and professor of biomedical engineering. Before that, he was vice dean for research at Johns Hopkins.

Dr. Zerhouni was born in Nedroma, Algeria, and came to the United States at age 24, having earned his medical degree at the University of Algiers School of Medicine in 1975. After completing his residency in diagnostic radiology at Johns Hopkins in 1978 as chief resident, he served as assistant professor in 1979 and associate professor in 1985. Between 1981 and 1985 he was in the Department of Radiology at Eastern Virginia Medical School and its affiliated DePaul Hospital. In 1988, Dr. Zerhouni returned to Johns Hopkins where he was appointed director of the MRI division, and then was appointed full professor in 1992, becoming the chairman of the radiology department in January 1996.

Since 2000, he has been a member of the National Academy of Sciences' Institute of Medicine. He served on the National Cancer Institute's Board of Scientific Advisors from 1998–2002. In 1988, he was a consultant to the World Health Organization, and in 1985 he was a consultant to the White House under President Ronald Reagan.

A resident of Baltimore, he has won several awards for his research including a Gold Medal from the American Roentgen Ray Society for CT research and two Paul Lauterbur Awards for MRI research. His research in imaging led to advances in Computerized Axial Tomography (CAT scanning) and Magnetic Resonance

Imaging (MRI) that resulted in 157 peer-reviewed publications and 8 patents.

WORKSHOP PARTICIPANTS

A complete list of the names and affiliations of the 200 workshop participants is available at <http://www.nationalacademies.org/moreworkshop>.

Appendix C

Biographical Sketches of Planning Committee and Staff

CO-CHAIRS

Anthony L. DePass is the associate dean of research and associate professor of biology at the Brooklyn campus of Long Island University (LIU). He is the principal investigator (PI) and director of the MBRS SCORE program at LIU; he is also the co-PI and a member of the administrative core of an NIH/NCI funded partnership between LIU and Columbia University that addresses cancer-related health disparities.

Dr. DePass' background in the areas of student and faculty development is quite extensive. He was the PI and co-director of the Multimedia and Interactive Learning (MIL) project. The NSF-funded MIL Project trained math and science faculty from five institutions in the New York metropolitan area in the development and utilization of multimedia applications designed to enhance the active role of students in the learning process. As chair of the Minority Affairs Committee for the American Society for Cell Biology (ASCB) and former chair of a similar committee for the American Society of Plant Biology, Dr. DePass has provided leadership in coordinating activities at the national level that are aimed at increasing under-represented minority representation within the scientific workforce. This work is supported by the respective societies in addition to a MARC grant from NIH/NIGMS awarded to ASCB for which he serves as the PI. Dr. DePass has served on several review panels and advisory committees that focus on the issue of underrepresentation of minorities in the sciences.

Originally trained as a plant biologist, Dr. DePass currently directs a funded research program that explores cancer-related gene regulation. His laboratory provides training for students at the high school, bachelor's, and master's levels, among which several students from underrepresented minorities have gone onto competitive doctoral programs.

Larry V. Hedges is the Board of Trustees Professor of Statistics and Social Policy at Northwestern University, the university's most distinguished academic position. He is also a Faculty Fellow with the Institute for Policy Research at Northwestern. He was previously the Stella M. Rowley Distinguished Service Professor of Education, Psychology, and Sociology at the University of Chicago. Dr. Hedges' research straddles sociology, psychology, and educational policy. He is best known for his work to develop statistical methods for meta-analysis (a statistical analysis of the results of multiple studies that combines their findings) in the social, medical, and biological sciences. Examples of some his recent studies include: understanding the costs of generating systematic reviews, differences between boys and girls in mental test scores, the black-white gap in achievement test scores, and frameworks for international comparative studies on education. He has authored or co-authored numerous journal articles and five books, including the seminal *Statistical Methods for Meta-Analysis* (with I. Olkin) and *The Handbook of Research Synthesis* (with H. Cooper). He has been elected a member or fellow of numerous boards, associations, and professional organizations, including the National Academy of Education, the American Statistical Association, the American Psychological Association, and the Society of Multivariate Experimental Psychology and chaired the Technical Advisory Group of the U.S. Department of Education's What Works Clearinghouse. Dr. Hedges holds a BA in mathematics from the University of California, San Diego, and an MA in statistics and PhD in mathematical methods in educational research from Stanford University.

MEMBERS

Daryl E. Chubin became founding director of the AAAS Center for Advancing Science & Engineering Capacity at the American Association for the Advancement of Science in August 2004. Prior to that, he served more than three years as senior vice president, research, policy & programs at the National Action Council for Minorities in Engineering (NACME) in White Plains, New York, after nearly 15 years in federal service. Government posts included senior policy officer for the National Science Board at the National Science Foundation (NSF) (1998–2001); division director for research, evaluation and communication in NSF's Directorate for Education and Human Resources (1993–1998); and (on detail) assistant director for social and behavioral sciences (and education) at the White House Office of Science and Technology Policy (1997). He began his federal career in 1986 at the congressional Office of Technology Assessment.

Dr. Chubin earned a PhD in sociology from Loyola University (Chicago) in 1973 and served on the faculty of four universities, including Georgia Tech, where he was promoted to full professor. He has published eight books and numerous policy reports, articles, and commentaries on issues in science policy, career development, program evaluation, and engineering education. Dr. Chubin's honors include AAAS Fellow, past chair of the AAAS section on Societal Impacts of Science and Engineering, Fellow of the Association for Women in Science, member of the National Academy of Engineering's Committee on Diversity in the Engineering Workforce, Integrator for BEST (Building Engineering and Science Talent), Quality Education for Minorities/Math Science Engineering 2006 Giant of Science, and Sigma Xi Distinguished Lecturer 2007–2009.

Howard H. Garrison has been the director of the Office of Public Affairs at the Federation of American Societies for Experimental Biology (FASEB) since the office was created in 1996. He is also FASEB's deputy executive director for policy. He previously directed FASEB's Office of Policy Analysis and Research and was group manager for the Survey and Evaluation Services Unit for Aspen Systems Corporation, staff officer for the Institute of Medicine's Committee on Biomedical and Behavior Research Personnel, and statistician with the Federal Personnel and Compensation Division for the U.S. General Accounting Office. Trained as a sociologist, Dr. Garrison has experience in biomedical research policy, statistical analysis, scientific workforce analysis, program evaluation, and surveys for agencies including NSF and NIH. He is currently vice president and member of the Board of Directors for the Commission on Professionals in Science and Technology, past president of the District of Columbia Sociological Society, and a former member of the NIH Minority Access to Research Careers Study Advisory Group. Dr. Garrison earned his AB from the University of Michigan and MS and PhD from the University of Wisconsin–Madison.

Carol B. Muller is the founder, president, and chief executive officer of MentorNet, *The E-Mentoring Network for Diversity in Engineering and Science*. MentorNet (www.MentorNet.net) is a nonprofit organization headquartered in San José, California. Founded in 1997, its mission is to further the progress of women and others underrepresented in scientific and technical fields through the use of a dynamic, technology-supported mentoring network; and to advance individuals and society, and enhance engineering and related sciences, by promoting a diversified, expanded, and talented global workforce. She is responsible for establishing and implementing the vision for the organization and its programs, developing needed resources, and managing those resources with the help of staff, volunteers, and partners to produce services of high quality and to deliver results. In addition to serving as MentorNet's president and CEO, she is a consulting associate professor of mechanical engineering at Stanford University. Both Dartmouth's campus-wide Women in Science Project, which Dr. Muller co-founded and developed when she served as associate dean for Thayer School of Engineering, and MentorNet have been recognized with the Presidential Award for Excellence in Science, Mathematics and Engineering Mentoring. She earned a bachelor's degree in philosophy and English from Dartmouth College, and master's and doctoral degrees in education administration and policy analysis from Stanford University.

Karen Kashmanian Oates is the immediate past provost at Harrisburg University of Science and Technology. In August 2007, she became deputy director for the Division of Undergraduate Education at the National Science Foundation. She previously spent 15 years on the faculty at George Mason University after a successful career as a research scientist in both private industry and at the National Institutes of Health/National Cancer Institute, where her research focused on the active effects and characterization of thymic hormones in immune restoration and cancer therapy. During her tenure at George Mason, Dr. Oates held several key leadership positions, including associate dean for the College of Integrative Studies (New Century College). She is co-PI for the National Center for Science and Civic Engagement, co-PI for Science Education for New Civic Engagements and Responsibilities (SENCER), and senior science advisor for the International Women in Science and Engineering program. She conducts faculty development workshops on topics including assessment strategies, service learning, community- and discovery-based undergraduate research, using research to inform curricular design, and pedagogies associated with learning communities. Dr. Oates was previously senior science fellow for the Association of American Colleges and Universities. She received her BS in biology from Rochester Institute of Technology and her PhD in biochemistry from George Washington University.

STAFF

Adam P. Fagen is a program officer with the Board on Life Sciences of the National Research Council. He came to the National Academies from Harvard University, where he most recently served as preceptor on molecular and cellular biology. He earned his PhD in molecular biology and education from Harvard, working with physicist Eric Mazur on issues related to undergraduate science courses. His thesis focused on mechanisms for assessing and enhancing the introductory science course in biology and physics to encourage student learning and conceptual understanding. Dr. Fagen also received an AM in molecular and cellular biology from Harvard, based on laboratory research in molecular evolutionary genetics, and a BA from Swarthmore College with a double-major in biology and mathematics. In addition to genetics and molecular biology, he is interested in improving undergraduate and graduate science education and other scientific workforce and policy issues. He served as co-director of the 2000 National Doctoral Program Survey, an online assessment of doctoral programs organized by the National Association of Graduate-Professional Students and supported by the Alfred P. Sloan Foundation.

Since coming to the National Academies, Dr. Fagen was study director for *Bridges to Independence: Fostering the Independence of New Investigators in Biomedical Research* (2005) and co-study director for *Treating Infectious Diseases in a Microbial World: Report of Two Workshops on Novel Antimicrobial Therapeutics* (2006). He is study director or staff officer for several ongoing projects, including the National Academies Summer Institute on Undergraduate Education in Biology, A Leadership Summit to Effect Change in Teaching and Learning: Undergraduate Education in Agriculture, the National Academies Human Embryonic Stem Cell Research Advisory Committee, Biomolecular Materials and Processes, and Research at the Intersection of the Physical and Life Sciences.

Tova G. Jacobovits was a senior program assistant with the Board on Life Sciences of the National Research Council until June 2007. She joined the National Academies with an interest in science policy after an internship at the Department of State in the Office of Science and Technology Policy Adviser. At the State Department, her research focused on the methods used by the U.S. government to monitor international human subjects research. Ms. Jacobovits was first introduced to science policy through an internship with the American Association for the Advancement of Science in the Science, Freedom, Responsibility and Law Program shortly after she graduated from the University of Wisconsin–Madison, where she earned her BS degree in biology and Hebrew language.

Since her arrival at the National Academies in January 2006, Ms. Jacobovits helped support numerous projects and reports, including the U.S. National Committee within the International Brain Research Organization and the 2007 NRC report *The Role of Theory in Advancing 21st Century Biology: Catalyzing Transformative Research*.

Ms. Jacobovits left the Academies in June 2007 to pursue a PhD in nutrition at the University of Maryland. Her research interests include energy regulation, metabolism, and obesity; food and drug interactions; food safety; and domestic food and agricultural policies.

Jay B. Labov serves as a senior advisor for education and communications for the National Research Council. He also served for three years as deputy director of the NRC's Center for Education and was the study director and responsible staff officer for the NRC reports *Evaluating and Improving Undergraduate Teaching in Science, Mathematics, Engineering, and Technology* (2003); *Learning and Understanding: Improving Advanced Study of Mathematics and Science in U.S. High Schools* (2002); *Educating Teachers of Science, Mathematics, and Technology: New Practices for the New Millennium* (2000); *Transforming Undergraduate Education in Science, Mathematics, Engineering, and Technology* (1999); *Serving the Needs of Pre-College Science and Mathematics Education: Impact of a Digital National Library on Teacher Education and Practice* (1999); and *Developing a Digital National Library for Undergraduate Science, Mathematics, Engineering, and Technology Education* (1998). He has served as director of the Center for Education's Committee on Undergraduate Science Education and Committee on Science Education K-12, and of the National Academies' Teacher Advisory Council. Dr. Labov is currently the co-PI for a multiyear grant from the National Science Foundation to the Center for Education and an NSF grant to offer workshops to grantees of the NSF's Math/Science Partnership Initiative that will enable them to better understand and implement the recommendations in NRC reports on education. He also currently oversees the NRC's and National Academy of Science's efforts to improve the teaching of evolution in the public schools and a recently expanded effort of the National Academies to work more closely with disciplinary and professional societies on education issues.

Prior to assuming his position at the NRC in August 1997, Dr. Labov was a member of the faculty in the Department of Biology at Colby College (Maine), where he served two terms as chair of the Division of Natural Sciences, associate chair of the Department of Biology, and member of numerous college committees and panels. He taught courses in introductory biology, mammalian anatomy and physiology, animal behavior, and neurobiology. His research and publications in the life sciences have dealt with physiological and behavioral aspects of reproduction in mammals. He was responsible for developing and overseeing a partnership program for Colby scientists and teachers in four local school districts. Dr. Labov also has worked with many national organizations and professional societies to improve science education for both pre-college and undergraduate students. He received a BS in biology from the University of Miami and a MS in zoology and PhD in biological sciences from the University of Rhode Island.

Rebecca L. Walter is a program assistant with the Board on Life Sciences of the National Research Council. Ms. Walter is interested in biodiversity, conservation, and education. She joined the National Academies in 2007 after working as a zookeeper and lecturer for Clyde Peeling's Reptiland in Pennsylvania. Prior to living in Pennsylvania, she worked as a field instructor in Costa Rica, where she taught rainforest ecology and sea turtle ecology to high school students. Before moving to Costa Rica, she spent two years teaching English at an immersion school in Mexico. She worked for one year as a zookeeper in the Baltimore Zoo's Reptile House after earning her BA in biology at the University of Virginia in 2001.

CONSULTANTS

Steven Olson is the author of *Mapping Human History: Genes, Race, and Our Common Origins* (Boston: Houghton Mifflin), which was one of five finalists for the 2002 nonfiction National Book Award and received the Science-in-Society Award from the National Association of Science Writers. His most recent book, *Count Down: Six Kids Vie for Glory at the World's Toughest Math Competition* (Boston: Houghton Mifflin), was named a best science book of 2004 by *Discover* magazine. He has written several other books, including *Evolution in Hawaii* and *Biotechnology: An Industry Comes of Age*. He has been a consultant writer for the National Academy of Sciences and National Research Council, Howard Hughes Medical Institute, National Institutes of Health, The Institute for Genomic Research, and many other organizations. He is the author of articles in *The Atlantic Monthly*, *Science*, *Smithsonian*, *The Washington Post*, *Scientific American*, *Wired*, *The Yale Alumni Magazine*, *The Washingtonian*, *Slate*, *Teacher*, *Astronomy*, *Science 82-86*, and other magazines. In September 2004 he published with two co-authors an article in *Nature* that presented a fundamentally new perspective on human ancestry. From 1989 through 1992, he served as special assistant for communications in the White House Office of Science and Technology Policy. He earned a bachelor's degree in physics from Yale University in 1978.

Paula Tarnapol Whitacre has served as a consultant writer and editor for more than 10 years, working on print and online publications for organizations that include the National Research Council, National Institutes of Health, Resources for the Future, U.S. Agency for International Development (USAID), and The World Bank. Previously, she developed an international resource center for GreenCOM, an environmental education and communication project funded by USAID, and was director of communications for the Society of American Foresters. Ms. Whitacre is a former Foreign Service Officer with BA and MA degrees in international studies from Johns Hopkins University.